CAMBRIDGE LIBRARY COLLECTION

Books of enduring scholarly value

Egyptology

The large-scale scientific investigation of Egyptian antiquities by Western scholars began as an unintended consequence of Napoleon's invasion of Egypt during which, in 1799, the Rosetta Stone was discovered. The military expedition was accompanied by French scholars, whose reports prompted a wave of enthusiasm that swept across Europe and North America resulting in the Egyptian Revival style in art and architecture. Increasing numbers of tourists visited Egypt, eager to see the marvels being revealed by archaeological excavation. Writers and booksellers responded to this growing interest with publications ranging from technical site reports to tourist guidebooks and from children's histories to theories identifying the pyramids as repositories of esoteric knowledge. This series reissues a wide selection of such books. They reveal the gradual change from the 'tomb-robbing' approach of early excavators to the highly organised and systematic approach of Flinders Petrie, the 'father of Egyptology', and include early accounts of the decipherment of the hieroglyphic script.

The Royal Tombs of the Earliest Dynasties

A pioneering Egyptologist, Sir William Matthew Flinders Petrie (1853–1942) excavated over fifty sites and trained a generation of archaeologists. His meticulous recording of artefacts and his sequence dating of pottery types found in Egypt and Palestine made Near Eastern archaeology a more rigorous and scientific discipline. This fully illustrated follow-up report of 1901 on the royal tombs at Abydos, capital of Upper Egypt, covers the early dynastic period (*c*.3100–*c*.2700 BCE). Petrie gives detailed descriptions of eight tombs and the associated finds. A chapter on the inscriptions is provided by Francis Llewellyn Griffith (1862–1934). Petrie wrote prolifically throughout his long career for both specialists and non-specialists. His preliminary report, *The Royal Tombs of the First Dynasty* (1900), and the three-part *Abydos* (1902–4) are among those works also reissued in this series.

Cambridge University Press has long been a pioneer in the reissuing of out-of-print titles from its own backlist, producing digital reprints of books that are still sought after by scholars and students but could not be reprinted economically using traditional technology. The Cambridge Library Collection extends this activity to a wider range of books which are still of importance to researchers and professionals, either for the source material they contain, or as landmarks in the history of their academic discipline.

Drawing from the world-renowned collections in the Cambridge University Library and other partner libraries, and guided by the advice of experts in each subject area, Cambridge University Press is using state-of-the-art scanning machines in its own Printing House to capture the content of each book selected for inclusion. The files are processed to give a consistently clear, crisp image, and the books finished to the high quality standard for which the Press is recognised around the world. The latest print-on-demand technology ensures that the books will remain available indefinitely, and that orders for single or multiple copies can quickly be supplied.

The Cambridge Library Collection brings back to life books of enduring scholarly value (including out-of-copyright works originally issued by other publishers) across a wide range of disciplines in the humanities and social sciences and in science and technology.

The Royal Tombs
of the
Earliest Dynasties

W.M. FLINDERS PETRIE

CAMBRIDGE
UNIVERSITY PRESS

CAMBRIDGE
UNIVERSITY PRESS

University Printing House, Cambridge, CB2 8BS, United Kingdom

Published in the United States of America by Cambridge University Press, New York

Cambridge University Press is part of the University of Cambridge.
It furthers the University's mission by disseminating knowledge in the pursuit of
education, learning and research at the highest international levels of excellence.

www.cambridge.org
Information on this title: www.cambridge.org/9781108066129

© in this compilation Cambridge University Press 2013

This edition first published 1901
This digitally printed version 2013

ISBN 978-1-108-06612-9 Paperback

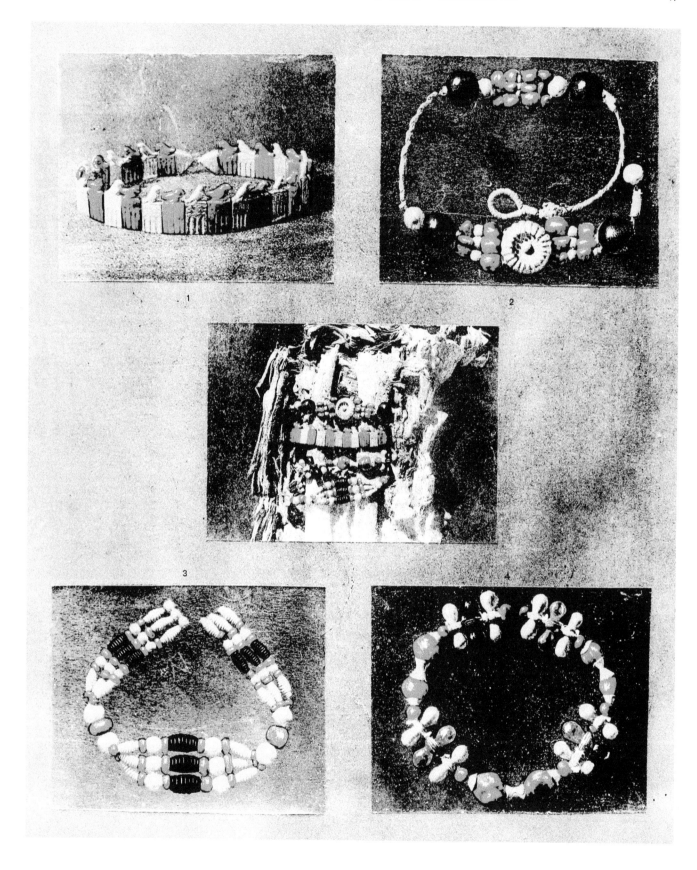

THE ROYAL TOMBS

OF

THE EARLIEST DYNASTIES

1901.   PART II.

BY

W. M. FLINDERS PETRIE

Hon. D.C.L., Litt.D., LL.D., Ph.D., Hon. F.S.A. (Scot.)

EDWARDS PROFESSOR OF EGYPTOLOGY, UNIVERSITY COLLEGE, LONDON;
MEMBER OF THE IMPERIAL GERMAN ARCHAEOLOGICAL INSTITUTE;
CORRESPONDING MEMBER OF SOCIETY OF ANTHROPOLOGY, BERLIN;
MEMBER OF THE ROMAN SOCIETY OF ANTHROPOLOGY;
MEMBER OF THE SOCIETY OF NORTHERN ANTIQUARIES.

With Chapter by

F. Ll. GRIFFITH, M.A., F.S.A.

TWENTY-FIRST MEMOIR OF

THE EGYPT EXPLORATION FUND

PUBLISHED BY ORDER OF THE COMMITTEE

LONDON
SOLD AT
The OFFICES OF THE EGYPT EXPLORATION FUND, 37, Great Russell Street, W.C.
AND 59, Temple Street, Boston, Mass., U.S.A.
AND BY KEGAN PAUL, TRENCH, TRÜBNER & CO., Paternoster House, Charing Cross Road, W.C.
B. QUARITCH, 15, Piccadilly, W.; ASHER & Co., 13, Bedford Street, Covent Garden, W.C.

1901

LONDON:
PRINTED BY GILBERT AND RIVINGTON, LTD.
ST. JOHN'S HOUSE, CLERKENWELL.

CONTENTS.

CHAPTER VI.

The Vases.

CHAPTER VII.

The Inscriptions.

By F. Ll. Griffith, M.A., F.S.A.

LIST OF PLATES

(WITH REFERENCES).

The plates i.—lxiii., without letters, are given to all Subscribers.
The plates for Students, iiiA.—lviA., with letters, are issued in a Supplement, which can be ordered.

KINGS MENTIONED IN THIS VOLUME.

Tombs.

KA

ZESER

NARMER

SMA

1st Dyn. *Manetho.*			*Sety List.*	
1.	Menes	. .	Mena	= AHA — MEN
2.	Athothis	. .	Teta	= ZER — TA
3.	Kenkenes	.	Ateth	= ZET — ATH
4.	Uenefes	. .	Ata	DEN — MERNEIT
5.	Usafais	. .	Hesepti	= DEN — SETUI
6.	Miebis	. .	Merbap	= AZAB — MERPABA
7.	Semempses	.	Semenptah	= MERSEKHA — SHEMSU
8.	Bienekhes	. .	Qebh	= QA — SEN

2nd Dyn.				*Remains.*
1.	Bokhos	. .	Bazau	HOTEP AHAUI
2.	Kaiekhos	. .	Kakau	RANEB
3.	Binothris	. .	Baneteren	= NETEREN
4.	Tlas	. . .	Uaznes	SEKHEMAB, PERABSEN
5.	Sethenes	. .	Senda	KHA SEKHEM
6.	Khaires	. .	. .	KA RA
7.	Neferkheres	.	Zaza	KHA SEKHEMUI

THE

ROYAL TOMBS OF THE Ist DYNASTY.

INTRODUCTION.

1. THE present volume describes the continuation and conclusion of the work on the Royal Tombs of Abydos, begun last year. It has not been practicable to include every result in this account, as some classes of objects require more study, such as the carved slate fragments and the worked flints. Nor is there any special virtue in comprising the whole of my results in two volumes, when so large an amount of the material from the same site is still lying in Paris awaiting publication. But at least there is now issued every inscription, and almost every class of objects, which have been obtained in this final work of rescue by my careful workmen.

The production of ninety-eight plates is a matter requiring time, both for digesting the material into order from rough heaps of fragments, and for the merely mechanical labour of drawing. To carry out this, several workers were needed. Mr. Mace superintended the excavations, and so left me free to work out the piles of sealings, stone fragments, and small objects. I only occasionally saw the digging, mainly for planning the tombs of Den and Perabsen, the central chamber of Zer, and the south half of Khasekhemui; the rest were planned by Mr. Mace. My wife drew all the plans, besides doing much in sorting and arranging material. Miss Orme's help was more valuable than ever, as she developed all my photographs, and inked in fifty-seven plates of my pencil drawings, beside drawing marks on pottery and helping in sorting the stone vase fragments. Without her doing such a great mass of work, this volume could not have appeared till many weeks later. Miss A. Urlin sorted much of the vase fragments, and joined many complex fractures, besides doing a great part of the daily marking of objects.

The general course of work was, that I photographed in the morning, sorted and drew stone vases in the afternoon, and sorted and drew sealings in the evening; though each kind of work was also taken at other times.

The importance of the material for study makes it needful to thoroughly publish every fragment. But as much of it will only be wanted by specialists, and would not add to the general interest in the subject, we have had to divide the plates as in the publication of *Dendereh*. The large edition presented to all subscribers contains sixty-three plates, of which fifteen are photographs and forty-eight lithographs. Besides this the supplementary plates which are not of general interest number thirty-five, of which ten are photographs and twenty-five lithographs. These are all distinguished by

B

letters added to the numbers, and are fully described in the text of this volume. They can be procured either separately or bound together with the whole series.

2. Again a rich harvest of history has come from the site which was said to be exhausted; and in place of the disordered confusion of names without any historical connection, which was all that was known from the *Mission Amélineau*, we now have the complete sequence of kings from the middle of the dynasty before Mena to probably the close of the IInd Dynasty, and we can trace in detail the fluctuations of art throughout these reigns. The 166 plates of results from our work will need some twenty or thirty to be yet added to record the whole of the information, which no one could hope to have recovered two years ago.

And this recovery is not only after the removal of everything that was thought of value, both by the *Mission*, and also by the thieves of Abydos who did the work, but it is in spite of the determined destruction of the remains on the spot. The pottery jars were smashed, avowedly to prevent any one else obtaining them. The stone vases, broken anciently by fanatics, are referred to thus, " ceux qui étaient brisés et que *j'ai reduits en miettes* " (Amélineau, *Fouilles,* 1897, p. 33), and we indeed found them stamped to chips; the stacks of great jars which are recorded as having been found in the tomb of Zer (*Fouilles,* 1898, p 42) were entirely destroyed; the jars of ointment were burnt, as we read, " les matières grasses brûlent pendant des journées entières, comme j'en ai fait l'ex

périence " (*Fouilles,* 1896, p. 18) ; the most interesting remains of the wooden tomb chamber of Zer, a carbonized mass 28 feet by 3 feet, studded with copper fastenings, have entirely disappeared, and of another tomb we read " j'y rencontrai environ deux cents kilos de charbon de bois " (*Fouilles,* 1896, p. 15), which has been all removed. The ebony tablets of Narmer and Mena—the most priceless historical monuments —were all broken up in 1896 and tossed aside in the rubbish, whence we have rescued them and rejoined them so far as we can. In every direction we can but apply to the destroyer his own words concerning the Copts who left the remains, " tous brisés de la manière la plus sauvage " (*Fouilles,* 1896, p. 33).

Of new methods employed in this work some may be worth future use, such as the restitution of the forms of the stone vases by an adjusting frame, the clearing of the weathered stones by a filling of sand on the face, and the adoption of a complete mode of registering every wrought fragment from a tomb by inventory sheets of outlines (plates xxxii. to xlv.), which enable a general idea to be obtained of the contents, and the trial of any union with pieces elsewhere preserved.

As most of the tombs are diagonal to the points of the compass, it may be stated that the upper sides of all the plans here are called the north in the descriptions, except pl. lxii., the top of which is called east, as owing to the shape it could not be turned ; and the general plan, pl. lviii., which is placed with the west at the top.

CHAPTER I.

THE SITE OF THE ROYAL TOMBS.

3. The general periods of the different groups of tombs can be readily distinguished by the change in the character of the objects found in them. In the sealings, for instance, there is a class of animal-figure seals which are closely like the later prehistoric work; these are only found commonly in the B group of tombs, few in the tomb of Zer, fewer still in that of Zet. On the other hand, the seals of Perabsen and Khasekhemui are more nearly like those of the IVth Dynasty: and those of Perabsen are intermediate between the earlier style and that of Khasekhemui. From the objects alone, therefore, it is clear which are the earliest and which the latest tombs; while the relative positions on the ground show in most cases the order betweeen these limits. It is evident that the earliest royal tombs are the easternmost of the larger ones, and that the progress was to the west, planting the tombs alternately north and south of the middle line. Even without any internal evidence of the order of certain kings, we should place the groups in this general succession.

4. When we examine the details, the relative order is more closely fixed by the presence of re-used vases of a king in the tomb of a later king. So that if we ignore all historical lists we can restore the order of the tombs in the following manner, referring to the letters shown in pl. lviii. :—

B
O } by style of   order B } by re-use
Z } sealings,   Z } of vase.

Y   by sealings, between Z and T.

T
X } by re-use of vases.
U

Q   by position after U.

Raneb
Neteren } by re-use
P   Perabsen } of vases.

V   latest, by sealings.

Hence the order of the tombs is in a line westward from B to Y; then alternate on each side of Y are T, X, and U; Q is placed further west of U; and then, after a pause, comes P on the opposite side, and then V again opposite to P.

In this order we have not fixed the place of the separate kings of the B group, nor that of Hotepahaui, except that he is shortly before Perabsen. But so far we have been independent of the historical lists.

5. In the first volume of *Royal Tombs* we have already shown how this order of the tombs agrees with those which can be identified in the lists. Two more such identifications can now be added; for on seal 109 we read Zer—Ta, and similarly on seal 2 (vol. i.) we read Zet—Ath, thus corresponding to the Teta and Ateth of Sety's list. Of the tombs placed in order above we can then identify

O Zer—Ta=Teta, 2nd king,
Z Zet—Ath=Ateth, 3rd,
Y
T Den—Setui=Hesepti, 5th,
X Azab—Merpaba=Merbap, 6th,
U Mersekha—Shemsu=Semempses, 7th,

and I have shown how the early form of the second name of Qa—Sen—was mistaken for Qebh (vol. i. 23), and so stated in the list of Sety.

It is evident then that five or six of the eight kings named in the Ist Dynasty are identified here in the right order of the tombs. Hence it is to the group of tombs marked B that we must look for Mena and his predecessors; and it is in this group that abundant objects of King Aha are found. Hence Aha must be within a reign or two of Mena. Looking at the sealings, it is clear that the seals of Aha are more like those of Zer than are any of the other earliest sealings. Hence Aha would come to be identified with Mena, entirely apart from the evidence of the ivory tablet from Naqada, on which that identification has hitherto rested.

Here a question arises, How is it that objects of Aha should be so abundant at Abydos when his tomb has been already found at Naqada? Where was his tomb? at Naqada or Abydos? Now at Naqada were found many ivory labels of necklaces, mentioning the number of stones, and with the name Neit-hotep on the back. These probably belonged to a queen of Mena. And if we must fix on one tomb as that of Aha, and one as that of a connection of his, it would be the Abydos tomb which would be that of Aha, where several ebony tablets record offerings to him; and it would be the tomb with Neit-hotep's necklaces which would be that of a queen. Also it is far more likely that a tomb in the great series of royal tombs should be that of the king, and that a tomb apart in another cemetery should be for a queen of his.

Hence it seems that the facts as now known would show that Aha—Mena was buried in the royal series at Abydos; and that the tomb at Naqada was that of his queen Neit-hotep, naturally buried with vases and objects belonging to the king. Further, it seems not improbable that one of the sealings there found is to be read " the spirit of Neit-hotep," *ba Neit-*

hotep (see De Morgan, *Recherches* ii., fig. 559), and was the queen's own seal.

We may now consider this group of B tombs more in detail. We know of this age several kings whose works are ruder than those of Mena, and who therefore must be presumed to have preceded him in that rapidly rising civilization. But unhappily the contents of these B tombs have been so ruthlessly confused and destroyed by recent digging that the chance of recovering their history has been almost lost. The list of named objects associated with certain tombs is as follows (see pl. lix):—

Ka, pottery	.	.	B 7, 11, 15.
Narmer, jar	.	.	6.
„ sealing	.	.	17, 18.
„ tablet	.	.	18.
Sma, about	.	.	15—19.
Aha, vase	.	.	17.
„ tablet	.	.	18.
„ tablet	.	.	19.
„ gold strip	.	.	15.
„ *Bener-ab* objects.			14.
„ sealings	.	.	16.

There is also King Zeser (*Royal Tombs* i. iv. 3), whose simple title of *nebui* connects him with King Sma and the vases of Zer (pl. v. 13, 14), and who therefore must be placed also among the pre-Menites.

The position of King Sma is indicated in another way. Several toilet objects with the name of Neit-hotep were found in the graves of female domestics around Zer, but none of the seventy gravestones bear this name. It seems then probable that these were disused toilet objects of Neit-hotep, the queen of Mena, such objects having been passed over to her handmaidens, who died in the next reign—that of Zer—and had the things buried with them. Now on one of these objects of Neit-hotep (pl. ii. 11) there is apparently *nebui Sma*, and as Sma cannot have been the husband or son of Neit-hotep, he was probably her father. Hence we are led to place Sma as the immediate predecessor of Mena, who married his daughter Neit-hotep. The extreme rudeness of the sealing and pottery inscriptions of Ka certainly point to his being before Narmer. Hence we have the series :—

Ka,
Narmer,
Sma,
Mena,

with Zeser probably before Sma, and yet after Ka. How far can the tombs be identified with these kings? The general order is from east to west. Hence B 19 is probably the tomb of Mena; and it is in No. 19 and the tombs adjoining it (15, 17, 18) that the objects of Mena are found. And such have doubtless been scattered in throwing the contents of No. 19 into tombs already opened.

The objects of Sma are found about B 15, but on the surface, so that their place is not certain. There would be nothing against the tomb of Sma being B 15, next to Mena.

The objects of Narmer are found in B 6, 17, 18. The large jar in B 6 is not likely to have been thrown far, and might well have been turned out of B 10 in throwing the contents back. So great a king is not likely to have had so small a tomb as B 17 or B 18, where only small objects of his were found. So that B 10 has a better claim than any other to be the tomb of Narmer.

The tomb of Ka is certain, as it was still full of cylinder jars, many of which bore his name; and the only other things of his were found some on either side, at 11 and 15.

And as Zeser was probably after Ka it is more likely than not that B 9 was his tomb, the only dated object in which was a sealing of Narmer, who was probably his successor.

The whole of the three rows of private tombs to the east of these great tombs contained no name on the sealings but that of Aha—Mena;

and hence they seem to have been added in his reign as tombs of his domestics.

Moreover objects of Mena were in B 14, including three with *Bener-ab*, "sweet of heart," probably a queen or daughter of Mena; and other pieces with this same name lay near by.

The whole result of this inquiry, piecing together all we can, from the order of the kings, and the sites where their objects have been thrown, is thus :—

B 7   Ka
B 9   Zeser
B 10   Narmer
B 15   Sma
B 19   Mena
B 14   Bener-ab
B 16   Domestics of Mena

The two tombs unnumbered to the north of B 14 were cleared last year by Mr. MacIver, who found there pottery (see *R. T.*, i., xxxix. 2, xl. 8) with rough figures of a hawk like that on sealing 96, and a bit of a bracelet with what is probably the name Aha roughly cut. So probably these were of sons or brothers of Mena.

Thus we have reconstructed the list of Thinite kings before Mena so far as the facts allow, and perhaps so far as we are ever likely to ascertain them. The case would have been very different had these tombs not been so confused by the previous work here.

6. The facts about the second dynasty, the kings after Qa, must now be studied. In the tomb of Perabsen we found that there were buried with him vases of three other kings, which—by the unbroken rule here—are therefore his predecessors. Their names are Hotep-ahaui, Raneb, and Neteren; and it is certain that Raneb preceded Neteren, as the latter had defaced and re-used a vase of the former (pl. viii. 2). As on statue No. 1 (Cairo Museum) these three names are in the above order, and the succession of two of them is now proved, it is only reasonable to accept them in this order.

The only link to the list of Sety I. is that if these are the immediate successors of King Qa (who closed the Ist Dynasty), then Neteren is the king Baneteren of the list. As there is no contrary fact this may be accepted.

After these comes Perabsen, and therefore he would be the Uaznes of Sety's list.

Before Khasekhemui must probably be placed Khasekhem, whose statues and vases were found at Hierakonpolis (*Hierakonpolis*, pls. xxxvi. to xli.); if so he would be the Senda of the list, Sethenes of Manetho.

Then there remains but one name in this dynasty, Zaza, according to Sety's list, to be that of Khasekhemui. Now there seems reason for this king being the last ruler of the Thinite dynasties, as there is no royal tomb known later than his at Abydos. Moreover we meet in his tomb with sealings naming the "king-bearing mother" Hapenmaat. She seems to have been adored throughout the IIIrd Dynasty, and thus appears to be the deified ancestress of that dynasty.

Also a sealing of Perabsen was found in the tomb of king Neterkhet (opened by Mr. Garstang, working for the Egyptian Research Account); and this king is the same as Zeser on the Seheyl stele, the 2nd king of the IIIrd Dynasty according to Sety. This shows that there was no great interval between Perabsen and the IIIrd Dynasty.

The length of the IInd Dynasty in the copyists of Manetho would at first sight be longer. But in the version of Africanus, which is usually the best, Syncellus, his copyist, introduces two more kings from Eusebius; and we now see that this is probably an erroneous emendation. There is, however, a King Khaires, who may well be the king Kara whose cylinder Mr. Quibell found at El Kab (*El Kab* xx. 29).

From all these available facts it seems that we ought to restore the dynasty thus :—

Tombs.	Sety.	Manetho.
Hotep-ahaui	Bazau	Bokhos
Ra-neb	Kakau	Kaiekhos
Neteren	Baneteren	Binothris
Perabsen	Uaznes	Tlas.
(Khasekhem)	Senda	Sethenes
(Kara)		Khaires
Khasekhemui	Zaza	Neferkheres

We must note that Perabsen cannot be the same as Send, as there were different priesthoods of these two kings. There are, however, difficulties with the list of Saqqara; and we have to choose between that version, as against the list of Sety and the presumption that Khasekhemui was the last of the dynasty. The above list is all that seems authenticated on all sides; but it may have to be extended by later discoveries.

CHAPTER II.

DESCRIPTION OF THE TOMBS.

7.   The oldest tomb that we can definitely assign is that marked B 7 (pl. lix.), the tomb of King Ka.   This is a pit with sloping sides, about 20 feet by 10 feet.[1]   The thickness of the brick walls is that of the length of one brick, about 11 inches; and the soft footing of the wall and pressure of sand behind it has overthrown the longer sides.   The chamber has never been burnt.   The broken pottery mixed with the sand, which filled it, largely consisted of cylinder jars, like the later prehistoric form W 80 (see *Naqada*, pl. xxxii.); and these had many inscriptions on them, written in ink with a brush, most of which showed the name of Ka in the usual panelled frame.   There can therefore be no doubt of the attribution of this tomb.

The tomb B 9 is perhaps that of King Zeser, who seems to have been a successor of Ka.   It is of the same construction as that of Ka, and about 18 by 10 feet.   It never was burnt.

8.   The tomb B 10 appears to be the oldest of the great tombs, by its easternmost position; and the objects of Narmer point to this as his tomb (see pl. lvi. 1).   The brick walls are 5 feet thick at the end, and 7 feet on the long side. The batter is 9 inches at the end, and 12 inches in the sides.   Thus in both the thickness and the batter of the walls there is a care shown in proportioning the strength of the ends and the sides.   The size is about 26 feet by 16 feet, and the depth $10\frac{1}{2}$ feet.   There are two holes in the floor, one being at the middle of each long side; and two other holes between these and the south corners : so it seems that there were five

posts on each long side, and probably one in the middle of each end, to carry the wooden roof. This tomb was never burnt.

9.   The tomb B 15 is probably that of King Sma (see pl. lvi. 2).   Its walls are not quite so thick, being 50 inches at the end.   The size is about 26 feet by 16 feet; and there is a large batter of 14 inches in the sides, and 12 inches in the ends.   The depth is $13\frac{1}{2}$ feet.   The post holes in the floor suggest that there were five on the long side, and one in the middle of each end, as in the tomb of Narmer.   But along the sides are holes for roofing beams near the top of the wall (lower sides at 149 from the floor, the wall being 160 to 170 inches high); they are drawn here on the east side, but others on the west were mostly broken away and inaccessible.   These roof beams do not at all accord with the posts; and this proves that, here at least, the posts were for backing a wooden chamber inside the brick chamber.   If this be the case here it was probably also true in Narmer's tomb; and hence these brick tombs were only the protective shell around a wooden chamber which contained the burial.   This same system is known in the Ist Dynasty tombs, and we see here the source of the chambered tombs of Zer and Zet. Before the age of Mena, the space around the wood chamber was used for dropping in offerings between the framing posts; and then, after Mena, separate brick chambers were made around the wooden chamber in order to hold more offerings.   This chamber was burnt; and is apparently that mentioned by M. Amélineau *Fouilles, in extenso,* 1899, p. 107.

10.   The tomb B 19, which contained the

---

1 The details of exact dimensions are placed together for comparison at the end of this chapter.

best tablet of Aha—Mena is probably his tomb; for, as we have noticed, the tomb with his vases at Naqada is more probably that of his queen Neit-hotep.

The length of the tomb is about 26 feet, and the breadth of it 17 feet; with a batter of the walls like that of the other tombs.

It appears to have had five posts along each side, like the other tombs.

As both of the tombs B 17 and 18, to the north of this, contained objects of Mena, it is probable that they were tombs of his family.

But the great cemetery of the domestics of this age is the triple row of tombs to the east of the Royal tombs; in all the 34 tombs here no name was found beside that of Aha on the jar sealings; and the two tombs B 6, 14, seem to be probably of the same age. In B 14 were only objects of Aha, and three of them with *Bener-ab*, probably the name of a wife or daughter of Mena, which is not found in any other tomb. In B 6 was a vase of Narmer, probably turned over from his tomb B 10, as B 6 is clearly of the same group as B 14, the tomb of Bener-ab.

11.   The Tomb of King Zer—Ta (pls. lx., lxi.), has an important secondary history as the site of the shrine of Osiris; established in the XVIIIth Dynasty (for none of the pottery offered there is earlier than that of Amenhotep III.), and visited with offerings from that time until the XXVIth Dynasty, when additional sculptures were placed here. Afterwards it was especially despoiled by the Copts in erasing the worship of Osiris. But of this later history the main remains were collected already by Améli- neau, and it is the early state of the place as the tomb of King Zer that we have to study here.

The tomb chamber has been built of wood; and the brick cells around it were built sub- sequently against the wooden chamber, as their rough unplastered ends show (pl. lvi. 3, 4); moreover the cast of the grain of the

wood can be seen on the mud mortar adhering to the bricks. The beams on which the wooden planking of the sides rested were 9 × 5 inches; of the 9 inches the wall end covered 3, and the mud mortar stood out 2 inches more, covering thus 5 inches, and leaving 4 inches wide for the footing of the planks. There are also long shallow grooves in the floor, a wide one (10 inches across) near the west wall, 3 narrow ones (2 inches across) parallel to that and a short cross groove: all probably the places of beams which supported the wooden chamber. Besides these there was, till four years ago, a great mass of carbonized wood along the north side of the floor, 331 × 36 inches, or 28 × 3 feet; in which were copper wire and nails. This was probably part of the flooring of the tomb, but it has entirely been destroyed after M. Amé- lineau uncovered it.

The floor of the tomb, beneath the wood- work, was covered with a layer of bricks 3 inches thick, which lay on 5 inches of clean sand. But all the middle of the tomb had been cleared to the native marl for building the Osiris shrine, of which some fragments of sculp- ture in hard limestone are now all that remain.

The size over all of the wooden chamber must have been about 28 feet square; the whole space including the cells around being about 43 feet × 38 feet. The best preserved parts of the wall are 9 feet high, and it is 8½ feet thick.

A strange feature here is that of the red recesses, such as I have described last year in the tomb of Zet. The large ones are on the west wall, and in the second cell on the north wall. Beside these, there are very shallow ones on each side of each of the cell walls on the north and south, except the eastern narrow cell on the north, and the two most eastern ones on the south; there is also one niche in a cell on the east. No meaning can yet be assigned to these, except as spirit-entrances to the cells of offerings, like the false doors in tombs of the Old Kingdom.

In the north-west corner of the tomb, a stairway of bricks was roughly inserted in later times in order to give access to the shrine of Osiris. That this is not an original feature is manifest: the walls are burnt red by the burning of the tomb, while the stairs are built of black mud brick with fresh mud mortar smeared over the reddened wall; also the bricks of the tomb are 9½ inches long, those of the stairs are 14 inches long.

In the narrow chamber at the head of this stair we found several jars of the Aegean type (base of pl. liv.) remaining perfect, with carbonized cloth; these are noticed with pl. liv. The later stairway was entirely removed in order to recover the early remains, including the beautifully engraved ivory box, pl. v. 4, xxxv. 13, which was under the stairs.

It is notable that the burning of these tombs took place before the re-use in the XVIIIth Dynasty; as is also seen by the rebuilt doorway of the tomb of Den (pl. lvi. 6), which is of large black bricks over smaller red burnt bricks. It is therefore quite beside the mark to attribute this burning to the Copts.

The great ranks of graves of domestics around this tomb had been nearly all cleared out by the plunderers of the past; and only a few objects were found in them, such as the ivory lions (pl. vi. 34) in O 29; the copper tools (pl. vi. 23—26) in O 31; the gold pin and tablet (pl. vA. 6, 7), etc.

12. The tomb of King Den—Setui was partially cleared last year around the smaller graves on the N.E. and S.W.; it has now been completely examined. The plan given on pl. lxii. will be seen to differ considerably from that published by M. Jequier; indeed it is difficult to see how some of his imaginary details were invented. The irregularities of the building, the varying angles, and the curvature of the entrance and sides of the chamber, are all carefully verified. There are two systems of direction; (1) the entrance passage, the eastern chambers on eithor side of it, the north side of the excavation and brickwork of the great chamber; and the south-west step passage and chamber by it; the other system is, (2) the great chamber, the north and south rows of graves, and those to the west.

How can this error have arisen? The surrounding rows of graves are probably later than the setting out of the great chamber, later, that is, by some hours or perhaps days. From the fact of the two stairways having the same bearing it is seen that their direction is not a stray error. It seems most likely that the stairways were first marked out by pointing to an object on the horizon, and the pit dug for the chamber. The error arose in making the south side of this pit not parallel to the north; the building was started on the south side, the north had then to follow that; the north and south rows of graves followed the sides of the chamber; while the east row had to be square with the entrance passage.

The length of the passage is 78 feet over all. Its general appearance in relation to the pit is shown on pl. lvi. 5, and a nearer view in fig. 6. The great brick chamber is about 50 feet by 28 feet, and 20 feet deep. The recess at the east end of it is 15 feet by 5 feet.

The astonishing feature of this chamber is its granite pavement, such considerable use of granite being quite unknown until the step pyramid of Saqqara, early in the IIIrd Dynasty. At first sight it might here be connected with the repairs of this tomb under Aahmes II.; but I found that the casts of stone vases (of the Ist Dynasty forms) yet remained upon the granite, proving that it was a part of the original tomb. Of this paving but few blocks remain; one at the west end, three at the north side, three or four lying loose, one threshold, and three small blocks in the south-west chamber. The western block, with a groove cut along it, is shown in photographs, pl. lviA. 1, 2. Around the sides of the chamber is a flooring of bricks, bordering the granite floor, as seen in pl. lviA. 1; these are laid as three lengths and one breadth, making up 27 inches width of brick bordering. At the north side the brick border is 16 inches wide. Some of the slabs are of grey gneissic granite, which splits into thin masses, the western slab being 111 × 64 inches, and only 5 inches thick; other slabs are of hammer-dressed massive pink granite. The blocks on the north side are (1) 53 × 28, running 6 inches under the east wall; (2) 98 × 28; (3) 52 + x × 27 inches. That there were other blocks is clear by the cast of a block remaining against the side of this line of blocks. The eastern recess of the chamber was, however, all paved with brick, like the bordering of the pavement on the other sides. A block lying in the middle of the chamber is 55 + x × 47 × 10 inches thick; it has been called an uninscribed stele, but is clearly a paving stone. The stele of Den was probably of limestone, like those of Zer and Zet, as the back of a limestone stele with rounded top, 21·6 inches wide, is lying in the tomb of Den.

Having now described what is left of the granite, we turn to the traces of the structure over it. Upon the three northern granite blocks traces remain of the wooden structure, casts of two beams, two planks, and seven post ends. It will be best if I describe the structure which they prove to have existed, rather than state the details. Against the north wall was a timber side, of planks laid horizontally, the outer skin 3 inches thick, the inner 2 inches; it is possible, however, that one cast might be due to a plank dropping out of place, so that there may have been only one skin 2 or 3 inches thick. These horizontal planks were fastened to upright posts to maintain them; the posts were on the inner side, and were much like modern joists, 3 × 10 inches, with the narrow edge against the planks; and they were at intervals of about 35 inches. Having thus faced the brick wall, much like a modern timbering of an earth face

in excavations, a second such timbering was built to form the chamber side, with the joist uprights towards the other joists, and the smooth plank face forming the inside of the chamber. The space in which the joists stood between the outer and inner plank facings was 38 inches wide. This space, partially divided by the upright joists, was floored over with brickwork on the granite, 5 inches thick. And in the space were placed large quantities of stone bowls and vases. In the burning of the tomb, the resins, ointment, &c., which were in these, melted and ran out, forming a paste with the mud, and so the vases became bedded. Afterwards these stone vases were all removed, probably at the time of clearing out the tomb and rebuilding the door jambs, a restoration which is dated by a piece of a stele of Aahmes II., found here by Amélineau. On the east side of the tomb there appears to have been only a single screen of planks, as a beam 7 inches wide is placed at the foot of the wall. It may be noted that the joists were roughly hewn at the lower end, of which the impression was left in the mud brick; and every joist had twisted on the base where it had no attachment, showing that it was firmly attached at the top. This twist, due to winding in the wood, is about 20°, and is exactly like that often seen in the posts supporting railway platform roofs. The twist was that of a left-handed screw in all cases.

The height of the chamber is quite unknown. The thick wall has a definite flat top, plastered over 259 inches (21½ feet) above the granite floor. This top has a sharp outer edge, which I carefully searched for, regarding it as a dwarf wall like that of Zet; but when it was defined it proved to be in line with the outer face of the thick wall where broken down; and hence it is the wall itself which was smooth plastered flat on the top, while a coat of mud plaster was also spread out eight inches lower than the wall, on the native marl, far beyond the wall, to the outer rows of graves.

The outside of the west wall was not found, so it is left in open outline. The spaces left white as chambers on the west wall were the remains of chambers built on the wall, which is continuous below them.

At the south-west corner is a strange annex, the irregularity of which gave some trouble. A stairway leads down from the west and then turns to the north; this lower end of it is shown in pl. lviA. 3, 4. At the foot of the first flight of steps is a space for inserting planks and brickwork to close the chamber, like the blocking of the door of the tomb of Azab (*R.T.* i., lxi.). This small chamber below was therefore intended to be closed. In the chamber itself were three blocks of granite. One (20 × 29 inches) was still embedded in the floor on the west side (see cross shade on plan); and in the wall above it was the cast of a large post of wood of 12 × 14 inches. At the east wall, opposite to this, was a hole in the floor, and a block of granite (20 × 23 inches) lying by it, which fitted, and is therefore drawn here in place (see cross shade). A brick paving covered the north half of the chamber; the square hole in this has blocks of limestone foundation beneath, apparently to support a slab of grey granite (23 × 43 inches) of suitable thickness, which lay displaced near it. It seems then that there were three slabs of granite in a line, one of which certainly was the footing for a great wooden post, so probably the others were for a similar purpose. These three posts thus indicated must have carried a great weight, as there would be only 6 or 7 feet space between them and over to the walls. Whether this small chamber was for the burial of one of the royal family, or for the deposit of offerings, we cannot now say.

Of the various rows of graves around the great tomb there is nothing to record in detail. In two places, one in the north and one in the east row, a large block of limestone came in the way; it was left where it stood, and walls built round it.

The tomb appears to have been cleared out with a view to repairs in the XXVIth Dynasty; the door jambs were renewed with thicker bricks 14 × 7 × 5 inches, in place of the old bricks, 9·7 × 4·8 × 2·9 inches; and the crumbling bricks burnt red were thus replaced by black brick, which has never been fired since. But there is no sign of such repair having been carried out around the chamber, the sides of which are much crumbled away. The only dated example of late work here is the stele of Aahmes II.

13. The tomb of Perabsen shows a great change in form since the earlier series. A new dynasty with new ideas had succeeded the great founders of the monarchy; and three reigns had passed by before we can again see here the system of the tombs. Even the national worship was changed, and Set had become prominent. The type of tomb which had been developed under Azab, Mersekha, and Qa seems to have given way to the earlier pattern of Zer and Zet. In this tomb of Perabsen we see the same row of small cells separated by cross walls, like those of the early kings; but in place of a wooden central chamber there is a brick chamber, and a free passage is left around it communicating with the cells. What was the form of the south side of that chamber cannot now be traced, as, if any wall existed, it is now entirely destroyed. The entirely new feature is the continuous passage around the whole tomb; this reminds us of the continuous passage around that splendid rock-cut tomb of the Old Kingdom at Gizeh, known as Campbell's Tomb. Perhaps in both the object was to guard against plunderers entering by digging sideways into the tomb. The same principle is seen at Tell el Amarna where a passage thus runs round the royal palace in the thickness of the wall.

The central chamber is 24 feet by 9½ feet, and the outside passage around is 53 feet by 42 feet. The views of corners of the chamber are given in pl. lviA.; the view looking west along the north passage is in pl. lvii. 1; and the north end of the central chamber is shown in lvii. 2. The many holes in the wall there have been made by plunderers seeking for hidden treasure.

We did not find anything of importance in position; the names of three earlier kings on stone vases being only loose in the filling, and the two great steles lying under a few inches of sand to the S.W. of the tomb. In the central chamber Amélineau found vases of copper, of stone, and glazed objects, none of which are published. In the passage on the west he found a great quantity of pieces of stone vases, but neither are these published. The sealings which I found in this tomb are given in this series, pls. xxi., xxii.; and the few small objects in pl. xlv.

14. The tomb of Khasekhemui is very different from any of the other royal tombs yet known. The plan on pl. lxiii. is divided in two parts in order to preserve the same scale as the other plans; the numbering of the chambers will make the junction of the two parts clear. The length from chambers 2 to 32 is 103 feet; from 32 to 46, the central block, is 39 feet; and from 46 to 58 is 81 feet, making a total of 223 feet. The breadth in the middle is 40 feet. But the whole structure is very irregular; and to add to the confusion the greater part of it was built of freshly made mud bricks, which have yielded with the pressure and flowed out sideways, until the walls are often double their original breadth. Nothing could be taken as certain except the bottom inch or two of the walls, or the points of attachment of the cross walls to the side walls. It was only owing to this flow of the walls over the objects in the chambers, that we succeeded in finding so many valuable things perfect, and in position. Where the whole of the original outline of a wall had disappeared, the form is given in the plan with wavy outline.

As nearly all the contents of this tomb were removed by the French work in 1897, and have

been recorded with less loss than was the case with the other tombs, it will be useful here to give a summary of all the remains whose positions are known, from the French excavations of 1897, and my own of 1901.

Chambers 1—12. Sealings of yellow clay found here are of different types from those found at the opposite end of the tomb (55—58), and are distinguished in drawings 211, 216, 217, 218 (pls. xxiv., xxv.). In 1897 were found coarse vases in alabaster, and covers of limestone, which, however, would not fit any of the vases. Also sealings in black and yellow clays, metal tools, flint tools, and pottery.

14. Copper vases (as pl. ix. 13); table of offerings.

16. Vases of syenite (see plan), red marble, blue veined with white, porphyry, &c.

17. Large vases of red and white breccia, 200 vases in all.

18. In corridor opposite, two great jars of alabaster (see De Morgan, *Recherches* ii., figs. 822, 823), marble and alabaster vases, table in two steps, and fragments of inscriptions.

19. Copper needles, chisels, axes, vase with handle (*Rech.* ii., fig. 827).

20. Two copper axes, which had been wrapped in cloth (pl. xlv. 76). Cylinders of limestone, and spherical vases of breccia and of granite.

21. In corridor opposite, a complete deposit of copper dishes and model tools, see description of pl. ixA. Near these were six vases of dolomite marble and one of carnelian, with gold covers (see pl. ix. 3—10); and copper bowls and ewers (pl. ix. 13—15).

22. Flint knives, scrapers, axes, &c., in all 594 objects.

29 and onward, pottery jars filled with grain.

32. Five perfect jars, like canopic jars, in a wooden box.

34—36. "Ne contenaient absolument rien que je n'eusse déjà trouvé des centaines de fois" (*Fouilles;* 1897; p. 42).

37. Many hundreds of carnelian beads of spheroidal form, found under the wall in 1901.

38. Stone chamber. Fragments of vases of dolomite marble, beads and small objects of glazed ware.

40. Fragments of vases of alabaster and breccia, nearly all in wooden cases. Copper chisel in doorway.

41. Skeleton broken up by plunderers.

42. Contracted skeleton. These two bodies were doubtless those of domestics, like those found around other royal tombs.

43. In passage two bowls or cups of copper, pl. ixA. 2, 3.

44. Model chisels of copper, and diorite bowl, pl. ix. 11.

45, 46. Large pottery jars of offerings.

47. Some objects of copper.

47—54. Pottery jars with clay sealings containing grain and fruits; some jars placed in grain stored in large boxes.

48. Of the gold and sard sceptre (pl. ix. 1) the larger part lay close to the wall of the chamber, having been passed over within an inch or two by previous work. The shorter part lay near this in the doorway.

55. One or two packets of reeds.

57. Basket work, from seats, &c.

A great quantity of sealings of yellow clay were found in the last few chambers, and they had probably been all originally in the chambers 55—58. Black clay seals, mainly of the official of Hapenmaat (No. 210), were found in the other chambers 45—54; but the pottery found in 1897 had nearly all been removed or scattered.

The central stone chamber is the most important part of the whole, as it is the oldest stone construction yet known. The general view looking north is given in pl. lvii. 4; the closer view of the work in fig. 5, and the mode of stone dressing in fig. 6. The chamber is 207 to 211 inches long, and 121 to 128 inches wide, roughly 17 by 10 feet: the depth is nearly 6 feet. The courses vary two or three inches in different parts; but these, and all the exact dimensions, are given in the next section. The blocks of stone were all fresh quarried; being soft, and dragging under the tool, when dressed. The natural cleavages were used as far as possible; and often half a face will be a cleavage, and the rest hammer-dressed. All of the adze-dressed faces are entirely dressed. The adze had a short handle, as seen by the radius of curvature of the cuts; and the cutting edge was of flint and not of copper, as seen by examining the marks of dressing with a magnifier. The internal joints of the stones are not all square, but are frequently skewed. There is no sign of any roof; doubtless it was of wooden beams, and has been entirely destroyed.

The brick walls are at a higher level around the stone chamber. The floor of the stone being 0, the top of the stone wall is 69 inches, the floor of chamber 41 is 78 inches, the floor of the south gallery is 81 inches, the top of the walls in the south gallery 160 inches, and that of the walls by the stone chamber 161 inches. But these latter have lost, both by wear and by sinking bodily. The top of the west outer wall is 172 inches, and this is the highest and best preserved part. It seems then, that the generality of brick chambers were about 7½ feet high, and the stone chamber sunk 6 feet below the general floor.

The arrangement of the brick walls around the central chamber is strange; but it was very carefully verified by cutting back the masses of crushed brick to reach the original faces, of which only a few inches remained at the base. The cross walls of 34—36 were traced forward close to the chamber, and leave no room for a brick wall between them and the chamber. The very thick wall east of the chamber was also verified. Remembering that the chamber was probably roofed over flush with the floor level around it, it may be suspected that perhaps cross walls were put over the chamber opposite those of 34—36, so as to hide it and make it like a part of the chambers 1—32.

On the east side of the chamber a hollow has been cut out of the stone at 15 to 40 inches from the north end, for three courses from the top: 4 inches have been cut away at the maximum. This was probably, like the cutting away of some brick walls elsewhere, done to find place for some large wood coffin or other furniture which was too tight a fit.

The southern end of the tomb was walled up anciently at chambers 53-4. But it was clear that there were two doorways through the wall between 31 and 34, which were merely filled with fallen earth and bricks.

15. The principal measurements of the royal tombs are here stated in inches in the same order as the description which has just been given.

KA. B 7. N. 128, S. 126 (118 at base), E. 247, W. 246 inches. Probably 6 × 12 cubits.

ZESER. B 9.

Top .	N. 118	S. 127	E. 223	W. 240
Base .	109	120	218	223

This seems to be only a bad copy of the previous tomb in its dimensions.

NARMER. B 10.

Top .	N. 206	S. 204	E. 314	W. 322
Base .	180	181	—	304

Depth 126. This seems to be intended for 10 × 15 cubits, but the top breadth and the half-way length agree best.

SMA. B 15.

Top .	N. 214	S. 211	E. 328	W. 320
Base .	177	181	300	298

Depth :—
E. Floor, 0. Base of beams, 149. Top of wall, 160.
N. − 5.   165.

This again seems intended for 10 × 15 cubits.

MENA. B 19.

Top	N. 207	S. 205	E. 311	W. 319

This again seems intended for 10 × 15 cubits.

ZER.

Top .	N. 520	S. 519	E. 468	W. 468
Base .	512	514	460	458

Diagonals at top, 695 and 697, so nearly square.

The inner clear space for the wood chamber is,

N. 408   S. 406   E. 334   W. 338

North wall 100 high at best.

DEN.

Base .	N. 593	S. 596	E. 348	W. 348
E. recess	N. 61	S. 55	E. 183	W. 181

Depths :—
Level of top of wall: N.E. 245 ; N.W. 248.
Granite sill in passage, 0.
Brick on granite, N. − 9.
Granite paving, N. − 14.
Brick paving, N. − 15 ; S. − 16.

PERABSEN.

Top . .	N. 502	S. 514	E. 631	W. 629
Base, about	495	508 ?	624	623
Inner block		385	524	
Inner chamber	110	114		297

Diagonals at top N.E. 828 ; N.W. 787.

KHASEKHEMUI.

Stone Chamber :—

Top .	N. 128 Mid.	S. 127	E. 209	W. 211
Base .	125 121	122	207	207

	N.N.W.	Mid. N.	N.N.E.	Mid. E.	Mid. W.
Courses .	70	69	69½	68	69½
	59	57	58	57	57
	48	43	45	45	43
	37	33	35	33	34
	26	22	25	22	24
	13	12	13	10	15
	0	0	0	0	0

The depths of the building are already stated, and it is useless to give dimensions of the brick work, as it is so very irregular. For dimensions of other royal tombs of the Ist Dynasty see *R. T.* i. 16, 17.

16. The mean dimensions of the bricks of the tombs are as follow, in inches :—

B 15 (Sma?) . . 8·9 × 4·5 × 3
B 19 (Mena?) . . 9·6 × 4·9 × 3
   Zer . . . 9·6 × 4·8 × 2·5
   Merneit . . 8·8 × 4·5 × 2·4
   Den . . . 9·7 × 4·8 × 2·9
   Azab . . . 9·8 × 4·7 × 2·8

Mersekha . . 9·2 × 4·4 × 2·5
Qa . . . 9·9 × 4·9 × 3·0
Perabsen . . 9·5 × 4·6 × 2·8
Khasekhemui . 10·5 × 4·9 × 2·9

There seems in these fluctuations to be a slight lengthening, the first five averaging 9·4, and the latter five averaging 9·8 inches.

CHAPTER III.

THE INSCRIBED TABLETS, &c.

PLS. II.—XII.

17. The account of the various objects found in the tombs will be stated in the order of their publication in the plates, as that enables the reader to refer most readily either way between the plates and text.

Plate I. (Frontispiece). The most important discovery of this year is that of the jewellery in the tomb of King Zer, which belonged to his queen. While my workmen were clearing the tomb they noticed among the rubbish which they were moving a piece of the arm of a mummy in its wrappings. It lay in a broken hole in the north wall of the tomb—the hole seen in the top of the cell next to the stairway, in views pl. lvi. 3, 4. The party of four who found it looked in to the end of the wrappings and saw a large gold bead, the rosette in the second bracelet. They did not yield to the natural wish to search further or to remove it; but laid the arm down where they found it until Mr. Mace should come and verify it. Nothing but obtaining the complete confidence of the workmen, and paying them for all they find, could ever make them deal with valuables in this careful manner. On seeing it Mr. Mace told them to bring it to our huts intact, and I received it quite undisturbed. In the evening the most intelligent of the party was summoned up as a witness of the opening of the wrappings, so that there should be no suspicion that I had not dealt fairly with the men. I then cut open the linen bandages, and found, to our great surprise, the four bracelets of gold and jewellery, in the order in which they are shown upon the arm in the central photograph of the frontispiece. The

verification of the exact order of threading occupied an hour or two, working with a magnifier, my wife and Mr. Mace assisting. When recorded, the gold was put in the scales and weighed against sovereigns before the workman, who saw everything. Rather more than the value of gold was given to the men, and thus we ensured their goodwill and honesty for the future. The sequel is instructive. Though all our camp of workers knew about this and about several other finds of gold, yet the willing separation between our workmen (who came from Koptos, fifty miles away) and the local natives was so complete that no tales of the gold got about the country. When the Arabic papers copied the discovery from my letter in the *Times*, after I had left Egypt, it caused a great ferment in the neighbourhood, and huge tales of the gold and treasures rent the hearts of the local plunderers, who till then were in ignorance of the valuables that my men had found. There could not be a more satisfactory hold over the workmen than that which is proved by this whole affair.

The history of the arm can be somewhat inferred. It certainly had not been looked into by any one since the first plunderer, or the obvious lump of gold would have been taken. And the plunderers who broke up the body of the queen must have been later than those who hacked the holes in the walls in search of treasure. So we may reconstruct the history in this fashion. The roof of the tomb had become decayed and let the sand pour through, over the queen's body, before the first plunderers broke in to ransack the king's treasures. They made holes in the walls while probably standing on a sand heap, high up, in search of hidden valuables. When the tomb was cleared out for building the Osiris shrine, in the time of Amenhotep III. (for the oldest offerings are of his age, and none even of Tahutmes III.), then probably the body of the queen was found and broken up. One workman hastily put this forearm in the hole in the wall, and then either got so much more plunder that he ran away, or else perished in a squabble. This hole never seems to have been disturbed when building the stairway close by it; and for more than a thousand years offerings continued to be made here, and visitors passed within a few feet of the arm without looking at it. The Copts then destroyed the shrine and all that they could find, but never touched the arm. The *Mission Amélineau* cleared the tomb, but still the arm lay in the hole in the wall. Lastly my men eyed the gold, and preserved it with all care; and these bracelets will now be preserved in the Cairo Museum, until some future convulsion when they may share the fate which denies more than a few centuries of existence to any known treasure.[1]

18. We now turn to the details of the bracelets.

The hawk bracelet (pl. i. 1) consists of 13 gold and 14 turquoise plaques in the form of the façade with the hawk, which usually encloses the *ka* name of the king. The strip was set up for photographing with the inner side

---

[1] The last century has seen Napoleon's raids on artistic wealth, thefts from at least three national museums, the attempted burning of one great museum, the destruction of the gold in two provincial museums, and the entire wreck of everything in another important museum, without counting the looting and burning of the Summer Palace at Pekin. Such are the chances that valuables suffer when known. The printed description distributed in all the libraries of the world will last far longer than most of the objects themselves. To leave important remains without any diffused record is a crime only exceeded by that of their destruction.

outward, the order was as in the central photograph. Similar single pieces of lazuli and of ivory have been found loose (pl. xxxv. 81), showing that other jewellery of this design also existed. Whether the punched rectangles on the gold are to be understood as part of the panelling, or as a rough rendering of the spaces in the sign *Zer*, is not certain. On the plaques of turquoise, which are the older, the holes generally conform to the three grooves below, but on the gold plaques there is no conformity, and this points to their being copied from the spaces in the *zer* sign. The plaques have a system of numbering on the bases beginning with the largest, and proceeding in gradation to the smallest; half are numbered with upright strokes for one half of the bracelet, and the other half with sloping strokes. But 5 of gold and 4 of lazuli are missing; and 4 lazuli have no strokes, but by their size probably belong to the places marked with (?) here. The numbers still preserved are :—

Gold—
    Upright lines .. 2 .. 4 5 6 .. 8 9
    Sloping lines 1 2 3 .. 5 6 7 .. 9

Turquoise—
    Upright lines 1 2 3 4 (?) .. .. (?) ..
    Sloping lines .. (?) 3 4 5 6 7 8 (?)

The gold hawks have been cast in a mould with two faces, and the junction line has been carefully removed and burnished. They are alike in the height of the bird, and the width; but differ in total height from the varying depth to which the mould was filled at the base. The two horizontal threading holes were probably cast, as there is no tapering and no burr to them; but they are not all on the same level. The gold was worked by chisel and burnishing; no grinding or file marks are visible. The chisel used for surface work was ·035 inch wide; the punch was ·026 × ·016.

The end pieces are made as a beaten cone, flatted to an oval, and closed at the open end by a plate soldered in. Four thread holes were afterwards drilled in the plate, the burr of drilling still showing. The turquoise was cut with a saw, and worked over with a drill and a graving point. The drill holes for threading are conical, up to ·024 inch wide.

On examining the edges of the turquoise plaques there is seen on some of them a wear at a little distance from the threading holes, leaving a rise of stone around the hole. This can only have been caused by a large bead with a wide conical hole (such as the amethyst ball beads in bracelet 2) wearing on the turquoise. And it will be seen that the hawks on the turquoise are like those of Mena (see pl. iii. 1, &c.), while those on the gold are like those of Zer (see pl. v. 1, &c.).

Hence the history of the bracelet seems to be (1) an armlet or bracelet of turquoise plaques and amethyst (?) ball beads, made at the close of Mena's reign or beginning of that of Zer, very probably at the queen's marriage; (2) the gold hawks cast of a later style when the permanent type was almost developed, and the armlet threaded with gold and turquoise alternate; (3) nine of the plaques lost, and the rest threaded to the smaller size of a bracelet; for had the diminution been intentional the plaques would have been removed in pairs and not irregularly.

The interest of this beautiful bracelet is increased by its embodying the turning point of the crystallization of Egyptian style, containing, as it does, the archaic work along with that which is almost fully developed.

The second bracelet, with the rosette, is entirely different in design. The two groups of beads are united at the sides by bands of gold wire and thick hair, probably from tails of oxen. The plait was made with three gold wires, three hairs, and three wires, interwoven; but the hair is now so brittle that some of it is lost. The wire has been carefully wrought to just the same thickness as the hair, ·013 inch. The front group has the gold rosette in the middle; this is copied from the centre of the lotus flower, made hollow, and pierced with three holes at each side for threading. The middle plate has been soldered halfway down the cup of gold, and the edges then turned inward over it. The turquoises are irregular in form, but polished and pierced. The three gold balls which separate them, are hammered out, and then soldered together; but so finely that no trace of soldering can be seen and the only evidence of it is that the axis of one ball is slightly askew. The little spacer pierced with three holes next to the amethysts is hammered in one piece; like a similar spacer in the middle of the back group. The large ball amethysts are of deep colour. The fastening of the braclet was by a loop and button. This button is a hollow ball of gold with a shank of gold wire fastened in it; no trace of solder can be seen on examining the inside with a magnifier; but the perfectly tight union of the wire and the inside of the ball shows that it must be soldered.

The third bracelet is formed of three similar groups, one larger, and the other smaller on either side. The middle of each group consists of three beads of dark purple lazuli, a tint that I have never seen before in Egyptian use. These beads are carved in a spiral imitating the gold beads. The long gold beads are made by coiling a gold wire, which is wrought thicker at the end than in the middle, to harmonize with the barrel form of the whole bead. This is the same form as the large gold bead of the age of Mena found by De Morgan. The gold is so pure and soft that on parting the coils of one bead with the finger-nail to see whether they were soldered, the gap could be closed again by a simple pressure on the end. The gold balls are all wrought hollow, and the groups of three are soldered together. The smaller beads are of turquoise. The fastening of this bracelet was by a loop and button.

The fourth bracelet, with the hour-glass beads,

is again entirely different from the other three. The groups of hour-glass beads are each of gold on either side, and of amethyst in the middle, or in one case of dark brown limestone. Each bead has a double ridge around the middle of it, with a deep groove between. Two hairs were passed through the pierced beads, and then parted one on either side of the hour-glass beads, and lodged in the groove. The hairs were kept in place by binding them close on each side of the bead by a lashing of very fine gold wire. The turquoises are lozenge-shaped, with gold caps on the ends to prevent wear; the caps in the middle being each a double cone in one piece.

Such is this extraordinary group of the oldest jewellery known, some two thousand years before that from Dahshur. Here, at the crystallizing point of Egyptian art, we see the unlimited variety and fertility of design. Excepting the plain gold balls, there is not a single bead in any one braclet which would be interchangeable with those in another bracelet. Each is of independent design, fresh and free from all convention or copying. And yet not any one of these would be in place among the jewellery of the XIIth Dynasty; they all belong to the taste of their age,—the purest handwork, the most ready designing, and not a suspicion of merely mechanical polish and glitter. The technical perfection of the soldering has never been excelled, as the joints show no difference of colour, and no trace of excess. Happy is it that the exact order of the beads was fully observed, so that we can replace their original design and effect; so different from the fate of the Dahshur collection, which has been all confused, owing to being gathered together by ignorant workmen, and the value of it thus partly lost.

19. PL. II. 1. The earliest sealing found was that of King Ka, which differs much from all of the others in its simplicity. It will be noticed with the sealings on pl. xiii.; but from the photograph will be seen how small is the sole impression that we have. It is on hard black mud, and seems to have consisted of only a row of enclosures containing the name.

2. A fragment of a name appears on close examination to be that of Aha — Mena.

3. A fine jar of alabaster (see pl. liii.), partly broken, was found in the most south-western of the small B graves, and its inscription is shown here. The forms are coarser than on the slate carvings, but are very distinct: the hawk is much like that on the great slate; the deeply curved top is usual under Narmer, though only occasional under Mena, and then flatter, and is never seen under later kings. The fish is well figured, and the chisel is the true *mer* with excentric blade.

4. Two pieces of an ebony tablet (see drawing in pl. x. 1) were found recently broken in tomb B 18, and unfortunately the remainder is lost. The name was not seen until it was cleaned, owing to the coat of burnt resins which clogged it; the fish *nar* is clear, and the top of the chisel *mer* is just preserved. The fortified enclosure contains the sign *s*, and another which is new to us. The vase with wavy line on the lower piece is apparently intended for a stone vase of water, similar to that drawn on a tablet, pl. xii. 4.

5. A small piece of ivory has the name of Narmer engraved on it.

6. A fragment of an alabaster jar has the front corner of the name of Narmer, with the high peak like that on No. 3.

7. A piece of alabaster jar with a sign scratched upon it.

8. A piece of a basalt jar bears the name of the " double lord, Sma "; 9 shows the same on an ivory jar; and 10 the same on an ivory rod. This form of the title is rare, and does not occur later than King Zer (see v. 13, 14; xii. 1); it is also known as the title of King Zeser (Royal Tombs, i. iv. 3). But in later times it always has the vulture and uraeus upon it, as in the

many examples of King Qa (see pl. viii.). Apparently the same name is placed on the ivory lid of Neit-hotep, No. 11, for though irregular in form the sign is closely like the example No. 9. As we have pointed out in sects. 4, 9, this indicates that Neit-hotep was closely related to King Sma, and as she appears to have been the wife of Mena, this suggests that Sma was her father, reigning next before Mena.

12. An ivory jar of Neit-hotep found, with 11, in a grave of a domestic of King Zer; she had probably been a handmaid of Queen Neit-hotep, and so had received the disused toilet articles.

13, 14. These inscriptions, *as si*, are on hard pottery and alabaster, and should be compared with other early groups, *up as* (*Royal Tombs*, i.; iv. 5; here, xxv. 2).

15. An irregularly cut piece of serpentine bowl seems to have a part of the same group as on the sealing No. 113 (pl. xv.). These differ from the group of three birds on the vases of the Naqada Mena-tomb, as those always have small wings above the back.

20. Pl. III. 1. The large thick label of ivory has the hawk developing toward the later form, with the tail sloping down and a separate wing tip. The name of Aha is followed by the palm tree and heart, which often occur on small objects of this reign, see iii. 20; iiiA. 9, 11, 13; De Morgan, *Recherches* ii., figs. 813, 814. It has been well suggested that this is the name of a queen or daughter of Mena; and this name Bener-ab—"sweet of heart"—would be very probable; moreover, as these objects are all small pieces of ivory, they are likely to be from toilet articles.

2. (See also the drawing, pl. xi. 1.) An ebony tablet of Aha—Mena was broken in pieces in the previous excavations, and only the upper two parts have been recovered. This seems to have been an enumeration of captives, of which the number is lost below, but the name remains, apparently *Khent-ta* or Nubia, "the land of the

bow." The king is said to be *mes Anpu*, "born of Anubis"; just as on the other ebony tablets, iii. 4, iiiA. 5, 6=x. 2 and xi. 2, he is said to be born of Horus and Amiut (a form of Anubis). Then follows the name of a town or palace.

3. An ivory label apparently belongs to objects from Khent-ta, or Nubia. It might further refer to "wood from Sha," Pa-sha, a town of Upper Nubia (Br. Geog. 767), or Shat, a district of Nubia (Br. Geog. 774). This is from B 10.

4. The upper half of an ebony label, in good condition, is apparently duplicated in the lower half, 6, of a label now carbonized. In front of the name of Aha is a building with the *khaker* ornament. Next is *res meh shep*, perhaps receiving (captives) of the south and north. Below is a superintendent standing, and a man seated, apparently stabbing a seated captive in the breast. This suggests a scene of sacrificing captives at the royal funeral. Lastly is the title, "born of Horus and Amiut" (Anubis).

5. A well-cut piece of a dolomite marble bowl, with the name of Aha followed by *pa t*. Compare the fragment of a porphyry cup from the tomb of Den (*R. T.* i. xi. 7) with the same bird after the name.

7. The name of Aha on another piece of dolomite marble.

8. A piece of the top of an ebony tablet, showing the horns and ear of an ibex, and a branch (*khet*) bowl (*neb*) and numerals 23.

9—18. Small ivory labels, with signs incised, and, in one instance, painted (17). Three bear numbers ("100" on 9, "6" on 14, "8" on 16) like the labels with numbers in the Naqada tomb of Mena, though here these are too few to be the numbers of beads on a necklace like the Naqada labels. The hippopotamus occurs on No. 11, and the elephant on No. 18. The birds can hardly be identified in view of the diversity of drawing of well-known bird hieroglyphs at this time.

19. An ivory slip from an inlay with the scorpion holding a pick, like the scorpion tribal

emblem on the lower part of a carved slate at Cairo, showing the capture of towns.

20. An ivory comb, probably of *Bener-ab* (or *Am-ab*), a queen or daughter of Mena.

PL. IIIA.[1] The ivory slips 1, 2, 3, bear figures of captives, probably of Libyan race, and with these compare pl. iv. 3 to 6, and 12. The twist pattern of border is here seen on No. 1 to be as old as Mena, having the same mysterious crescents below it which even appear down to the XIIth Dynasty (L. *Denk.*, ii. 126-132).

4. An ivory hemisphere with the name of Aha.

5. See the drawing, pl. x. 2. A duplicate of this, much broken, is in No. 6, and a drawing in xi. 2. This ebony tablet of Mena is the most complete of his works. The lower half was found in tomb B 18, and at the close of all the work the upper half came from B 19. In the top line after the name of Aha, with the title, "born of Amiut," there are two sacred barks, and a shrine and temenos of Neit. The resemblance of this to a shrine on a cylinder, copied on this plate, should be noted. In the next line is a man making an offering, with two signs above, possibly *uāāu*, "alone." Behind him is a bull running over wavy ground into a net stretched between two poles, exactly the same position of the net as seen on the far later Vapheio gold cups. At the end is a crane or stork standing on a shrine. Compare with this the stork on a shrine, above an enclosure of wild cattle, on the mace head of Narmer (*Hiera-konpolis*, pl. xxvi. B). The third line shows three boats on a canal or river passing between certain places. It is tempting to see in these place names *Biu*, a district of Memphis (Br. Geog. 184), *Pa She*, the "dwelling of the lake," capital of the Fayum, and the canal of *Mer* or Bahr Yusuf (B. G. 278), divided in two, above and below

the Fayum. In the fourth line is a continuous line of hieroglyphs, the first of such that is known. The second version in No. 6, drawn in pl. xi. 2, shows that the second sign is not essential. On the backs of these tablets are painted signs: a spindle (pl. x. 3), and a *men* sign with two kinds of gaming pieces (pl. xi. 3).

7. A curved bar of gold was found in tomb B 18, the two ends of which are shown in fig. 7. The sides are even, and the whole is carefully wrought. Near the top is a hole, and below that the name of Aha incised. At the lower end is a close cross hatching, and the same is on the under side near the upper end. The purpose of it is entirely unguessed. It weighs 216 grains, a heavy example of the old standard for gold, known as early as Khufu.

8. An ivory figure of a girl was found in tomb B 14, possibly of the deceased Bener-ab, to whom this tomb apparently belonged. The dress is long, to the ankles, and the hands placed on the breast. It differs from any other figure yet known of this age; those from Hierakonpolis, with the mantle folded across the arms, being most like it. (*Hierakon.* x. 7, 8, 11.)

9. A polygonal slip of ivory, flat on one side, and with three faces on the other side, seems to imitate a flint flake. It bears the name of Aha, and pieces of other such models were found.

10. A piece of an ivory fish, similar to those from the Mena tomb at Naqada (De Morgan, *Recherches*, ii., figs. 702—707).

11. An ivory handle of a fan (?) having a slit cut along the widened end, has on it the name of Aha, and *Bener-ab*.

12. An ivory rod, bearing also the name of Aha.

13. A panel of ivory, probably from a box lid, with the name of Aha, and *Bener-ab*.

PL. IV. 1, 2. Pieces of alabaster with unknown signs.

3, 4, 5. Pieces of ivory with figures of a subject race doing homage. The pieces 4 and 5 may not belong together, but are clearly of

---

[1] All plates with lettered numbers are issued only as a supplement, which can be also had bound together in the volume. The more important tablets of this plate are also given in enlarged drawings on pls. x., xi.

similar nature. The long spotted robe is like that belonging to a conquering people on the slate palette with giraffes (Brit. Mus.).

6. Piece of ivory with figure of a subject bearing a stone vase on the head.

7. Part of an ivory bracelet.

8, 9. Pieces of ivory with parts of a figure and of a dog.

10. Piece of ivory box with name of Aha, and *Bener-ab*.

11. Piece of ivory decoration with figures of early huts. The sides appear to be of reeds or maize-stalks bound together; and the roof was probably of palm ribs interlaced and covered with palm-leaf mats, like the Bisharin tents of the present day at Aswan. These huts are like those shown on the mace head of Narmer, and on the long slate palette. The upper part of this ivory slip has the dome top of the hut and a subject bearing a branch, as in fig. 5 (see *Fouilles, in extenso,* 1899, pl. xlii.).

12. A figure of a Libyan captive on ivory, with the feather in the hair.

13. Unexplained fragment of ivory.

14. Flint arrow-heads from tomb B 18. Some dozens of these were found in the filling of the pit. Some hundreds had, however, been already removed in the French work, though unfortunately not one of them is now to be found in the Cairo Museum.

15. Figures of subjects bringing vases as offerings, on an ivory panel.

16. Piece of ivory with a part of a standard, from which an arm has projected holding a mace, possibly part of the group *Aha*.

17. Piece of ivory with a standard, from which is an arm holding a cord. Below is perhaps *ua she,* as on the slate palette of Narmer, " the prince of the lake," i.e. Fayum.

18, 19. Pieces of an ivory cup.

20. Slip of ivory with a row of five captives bound together; much like the work of groups of captives from Hierakonpolis.

21. PL. V. 1. Two pieces of an ivory tablet were so different in appearance that their connection was not seen until they were photographed. They seem to name " Hathor in the marshes of King Zer's city of *Dep,"* or Buto (Br. Geog. 939-41). The figure of Hathor with the feather between the horns is already known. This label may have been attached to an offering made from Buto at the royal tomb. Unless the continuity of the name can be disproved, it shows that Buto far down in the marsh of the Delta was already established at the beginning of the Ist Dynasty, and named after Zer, just as the farms and towns of the Old Kingdom were named after the kings who founded them.

2, 3. Small ivory labels, burnt. 2 names the commander of Zer's palace, *Zer-hor-ab;* and 3 may refer to the ruler of the Fayum, *ur she.*

4. A long box of ivory divided in two lengthways (see pl. xxxv. 13), has a similar inscription on either side, the better of which is shown here. It gives one of the best examples of the *zer* sign, and was found with other objects covered over by the brick steps of the XVIIIth Dynasty in the tomb of Zer.

5. A piece of a limestone vase names a man Neit-her.

6. A piece of an ivory wand bears the name Mer-neit; it may, of course, have strayed over from the tomb of that king.

7. Several ivory cylinder cups were inscribed for King Zer; this example shows how complete the style of drawing the royal hawk had become at this early date. The conventions are fixed in the final form which lasted down to Roman times.

8 is a small ivory label with a ram and an unknown sign.

9, 10, are wooden labels, respectively for arrows and for clothing.

11. Only a piece of one ebony cylinder for sealing was found, although thousands of impressions were placed in the tombs, from which over two hundred different seal inscriptions have been copied. This piece is about a third of a cylinder; it bears *ankh* and *mut* around the

top, and below that repetitions of a name or title written with *Neit, kh,* and two yokes.

12. A piece of a thin vase of crystal has petals carved in low relief on the surface; it is polished outside, but finely ground inside.

13, 14. These two inscriptions show the vases to have been used for the " washing of the hand of the double lord."

15. Other fragments were found of the strangely carved flat dish of dolomite marble, found last year (*R. T.* i. xii. 10).

16. Among the carbonized fragments was found a wooden carving of an ear of bearded barley.

17. A unique clay sealing with a very elaborate door pattern of King Zer is shown here.

18. The figure of a corded jar was engraved on a stone bowl, similar to the jar outline on pl. va. 24.

PL. VA. 1—5 are small fragments of inscription on stone and ivory; 4 and 5 being from ivory cups.

6. An ivory label bearing *up-as,* as on pieces 22, 23, and an uncertain sign below.

7 is a metal pin, apparently of base gold, as, though not bright, there is no trace of green copper corrosion upon it. The pattern of concentric circles round a spot also occurs on the early ivories, and therefore there is no ground for assigning this to a later age.

8. A fragment of an ivory tablet shows the king walking, and a small attendant following with a standard. Below is a canal.

9—12 are ivory fragments which do not fit any yet known. 12 seems to show the king on a throne and a lesser figure upon his knee, an anticipation, perhaps, of Akhenaten's family group.

13. A piece of an ebony tablet is scarcely legible. The enclosure contains apparently three bound captives.

14 is a square tipped rod of ivory, with the sign of the same, engraved upon it.

15—18. Fragments of ivory disconnected; possibly the remainders may be found in some other collection.

19, 20. Pieces of stone bowls with *du* (?) *khent* and *hotep.*

21. A piece of a stone bowl inscribed Merneit may very probably have strayed from the tomb of that king, as it is roughly incised like his other works.

22, 23, 24. Pieces of stone bowls, bear *up ast khent, up ast,* and the outlines of a corded jar.

PL. VI. 1. A fragment of an ivory bracelet, bearing *ankh* and *uas* alternately.

2. The head of a snake in ivory, carefully carved.

3, 4. Two lions carved in ivory were found in one of the private tombs around that of Zer. They are much worn on the bases by sliding about; and the lines of the fur are worn off by long continued handling just at the centre of gravity. It is evident therefore that they were playing pieces in some game, probably the same as the prehistoric game of four lions and a hare (see *Naqada* vii. 2). The form of the lion is more advanced than that of the lion found in the Naqada Mena-tomb (De Morgan, *Recherches* ii. 699); but the tail turns up the back with a crook at the end in the regular prehistoric mode. The two spots over the eyes of the lesser lion are not usual on Egyptian figures, but are known, I am informed, on Mesopotamian figures.

5—10. Some arrow-heads of crystal were found, and the handle end of a crystal knife. These do not bear the same regular and delicate work as the flint arrow-heads, and they are doubtless funerary offerings.

11—16. Flint arrow-heads were also found around the tomb of Zer, mostly of the same type as those of Mena. Two are, however, of a form entirely unknown as yet in any country (13, 14). The end is of the chisel form, and this passes below into the pointed form. It might be made with a view to a second use of the arrow after the tip had broken off in some animal; the detached arrow shaft would then retain enough flint to be quickly trimmed into a pointed arrow. The flint set in the wood did not seem capable of bearing any strain, but it was explained by my friend Prof. Giglioli as a tatuing instrument of the usual form. As tatuing was used in prehistoric times (as shown on figures then), and in the XIIth Dynasty (as shown by the body of a priestess at Cairo), there is nothing surprising in finding such a tool.

17. Model ears of corn carved in ivory were found, and other pieces are shown on pl. xxxiv. 82, 83.

18, 23—26. A set of three chisels and a graver of copper were found together in O 31, one of the graves around the tomb of Zer. The forms are such as we should expect then; the adze 23 being intermediate between the late prehistoric type and that of the IIIrd Dynasty. The signs on a chisel are given enlarged in fig. 18. The tools 23—26 are on scale $\frac{1}{2}$.

19—21. Pieces of elaborately carved broad bracelets of ivory were found, which from the uniform dead black colour seem to have been intentionally stained, and not merely burnt by chance. 19 has a twisted net pattern over it, and shows a trace of the name of King Zer. 20, 21 have patterns somewhat like those cut on the ivory slips (see pls. xxxiv. 53—55; xl. 56), but far more detailed.

22. A piece of ivory cup has a bold relief of a bull's head, full face, in a style very different from usual Egyptian work.

27. A small pink marble vase of the usual form is entirely covered with a carved net pattern in relief.

Pl. VIA. 1. Fragment of ivory label with the royal hawk, and *ha* signs.

2. Part of a label so similar to that on pl. v. 1 that it might be from the same source.

3. Sign on a panel of ivory. For such signs on stone vases see pl. xxv. 6, 7.

4. A piece of a wooden wand, now carbonized, with the name of Zer, and the jackal and dagger hieroglyphs, *anpu*, *tep*.

5. An ebony label with very roughly scratched signs that are not yet read.

6. The ivory lid of a slate palette for kohl, similar to that in pl. ii. 11.

7. Carved ivory bull's leg from a stool or casket. This is one of the most perfect examples of this type, which is found in most of the royal tombs (see pls. xxxii. to xliv.).

8. An ivory wand, complete.

9. Part of a figure of a hunting dog; probably a game piece, like the lions, pl. vi. 2.

10. Piece of an ivory vase with plaited pattern in bands.

11. Part of an ivory wand with animal's head. This bent form appears in the dancers' wands at Deshasheh (*Desh.* xii.).

12. Bull's leg in ivory.

13. Top of a chair leg in ivory, like those from the Naqada Mena-tomb (De Morgan, *Recherches*, figs. 689, 690).

14. Humerus of a dwarf; all of these are half scale.

15. Upper part of a chair leg of wood, originally covered with copper foil, as shown by the row of nail holes.

16. Lower end of a wooden staff, also covered with copper foil originally.

17. Slip of highly-polished cloudy agate, brown and white.

18. Clay sealing of King Zer.

16. Hollow frame of gold, forming a cap to some woodwork, which remained carbonized in it. It is closed at the top with a flat plate, and carefully rounded at the ends.

20. Handle to a saucer of ivory; others of the same pattern are found in carbonized wood. The end of the handle is sunk, and a groove runs up the side.

21. Cap of electrum, on which is minutely engraved the sign *ab*, the Osiris-wig standard of Abydos.

22, 23. Pieces of the dish with reliefs, in dolomite marble, like that in pl. v. 15.

24. Piece of dolomite marble, inscribed "libation to Anubis."

25, 26. Pieces of a tray of brown schist, elaborately carved with basket pattern.

22. Pl. VII. 1. Piece of serpentine bowl of King Zet.

2. Piece of a large and thick bowl of rough limestone of King Zet. Scale about one third.

3. Piece of ivory rod of King Zet.

4. Piece of dolomite marble bowl, inscribed for Zet.

5, 6. The only impression of the royal seal of King Den. The whole design of the seal appears to be, (1) The *ka* name Den with the hawk above. (2) The king standing. (3) An inscription, *em se ab en* . . . . *nebti*. (4) Den having hooked a crocodile is drawing him up out of the water, and preparing to spear him. (5) The king's personal name, *Setui* or *Semti*. (6) Den wrestling with a hippopotamus. A small part of such an impression was found last year, and was the first object which showed that Den was the name of Setui.

7. On a tall alabaster cylinder jar is an inscription in high relief, with the standard of the goddess Mafdet and the name of Den. This is the only such relief inscription yet found.

8. A portion of an ivory plaque shows around the edge the line of a fortification, implying that the whole subject is within a city. The gate with *khaker* ornament is seen at the left. Within the walls is a sacred enclosure with a ram in it, and a shrine, above which is a bucranion, similar to the doorways on an ivory carving from Hierakonpolis, surmounted with bucrania (*Hierakon.* xiv.); note the use of animal skulls for hanging up, by the "pan-grave" people (*Diospolis Parva* xxxix.). In 9 we see a part of a duplicate of No. 8, showing the king's name and title, and the head of a man. These plaques were smashed up in the general wreck of these

tombs by the *Mission Amélineau*, like so many other precious records.

10. The upper part of the finely-engraved crystal vase, figured in *Royal Tombs* i. vii. 4, was found this year. The whole group can now be restored. The lioness goddess Mafdet is standing holding an *uas* sceptre, beneath her is the title "mistress of the house of life."

11. Another fragment of a wooden tablet of Den does not seem to join any of those already published last year, but it is a duplicate of that figured in *R. T.* i. xi. 4 and xv. 18, in part, and probably in the whole.

12. A small ivory panel from a box bears the most crisp and fine cutting of this reign. Beside the name of Den there is the uraeus of judgment, the sign of gold, and the sign of a seal. The latter is instructive, as hitherto that hieroglyph has been taken to be a figure of a finger ring, but such a ring is quite unknown at this age, and the base of it is far too long for a bezel of any period. It is clearly the figure of a signet cylinder rolling on the clay. This group suggests that the box had contained the golden seal of judgment of King Den.

13. A cylinder of ivory has the lower end polished quite flat, and the upper end slightly coned and pierced with a small hole in the axis. It is exactly adapted for the handle of a measuring cord. On it is the hieroglyph of a measuring cord, and the king's name, Setui.

Pl. VIIA. 1. Fragments of an ivory tablet, with the king holding turns of cord on his arm; his name above, Setui; and the jackal standard in front. It may be part of one found last year (*R. T.* i. xi. 8 and xiv. 8).

2. A piece of an ebony tablet. The three signs in the fortified enclosure may perhaps be the same as on the tablet pl. vA. 13.

3. A fragment which is a duplicate of the piece in *R. T.* i. xi. 5 and xiv. 12, with the title *mes Tehuti*, like *mes Anpu*, &c.

4. An ebony fragment which seems to be a

duplicate of the left-hand side of tablet *R. T.* i. xi. 14 and xv. 16.

5. A fragment of tablet of the same style as *R. T.* i. xl. 6.

6. A fragment which might by the work belong to *R. T.* i. xi. 5.

7. A group of bows and arrows was found in one of the private graves west of that of Den. The bows are formed of two long straight horns of the oryx, fastened together by a tapered plug of wood in the cores; doubtless binding round the horns secured them from splitting. The wooden plug is seen just below the two top horns. The arrows are long bone points set in reed shafts, with a notch for the bow-string cut just below a knot in the reed.

8—13. Fragments of carved wood now carbonized were found in the tomb of Den. No. 13 shows the shoulder and arm of the king grasping a group of emblems, including a ring and a *dad* sign: or possibly the hand held a staff, and a group of lotus flowers stood before the king as on the slab of Men-kau-hor in Paris.

14. A piece of ivory inlay has the sign *ankh* upon it, of which half the bow and one end of the tie remain.

15. A bull's leg in ivory shows a clumsier style than that of the reign of Zer (viA. 7).

16. A perfect jar of slate, found in grave T 5, has two signs upon it, which are similar to those on the pottery.

17. Several signs are scratched upon alabaster: a group of three *neter* signs can alone be read.

23. PL. VIII. 1—4. Some weathered ivory labels were picked up by our workmen from the loose rubbish that had been thrown out of tombs. Four of these are of King Qa, No. 3 being repeated in drawing in pl. xii. 6. It will be seen how the name *sen* on these has the sign of breath (the nose) as a determinative. From a comparison of these tablets the separate groups can be cleared up, when the serious study of these inscriptions is undertaken.

5. This piece of a tablet appears to be of King Mersekha—Semempses, as it is a duplicate of that found last year, figured in *R. T.* i. xii. 1 and xvii. 26.

6. Inscription on stone bowl; compare *R. T.* i. viii. 9.

7. Inscription on stone bowl, joining that published in *R. T.* i. ix. 10.

8—10. Inscriptions of Hotep-ahaui on stone bowls. These show that the signs are not *sekhem*, as was supposed from the engraving on the statue No. 1, Cairo Museum; but from the open tops these must be *aha*. In no case on the sealings showing the *sekhem* sign (pls. xxiii., xxiv.) is the top divided in this manner. The name of the tomb is given as "the house of the *Ka* of the Horus Hotep-ahaui."

11. On this piece—found like the Nos. 8—13 in the tomb of Perabsen—we see another tomb name, which is probably a fuller form of that above named, but which might belong to either of the following kings: it reads "the house of the *Ka* of . . . . called *Neterakhet*" or "the divine glory." This is approaching the type of the pyramid names of the Old Kingdom.

12. A piece of a bowl of grey volcanic rock, originally inscribed for "the palace of the Horus Ra-neb called Sa-ha . . . ." This name is of the same type as those of the palaces of kings Qa (*Sa-ha-neb*), and king Hotep-ahaui (*Sa-ha-ka*). This inscription has been erased by his successor; showing that this was not inscribed for the tomb, but for the palace, and so left in use till the next reign. The later inscription is of the king Neteren, the third of those on statue No. 1. From this we see that this bowl was used for the king's "washing every day," like the bowls and jars for the king's hands, pl. v. 13, 14, xii. 1, xxv. 1.

13. Another piece of bowl was carefully inscribed for king Neteren. The presence of the boat here alone, and the instances of specific use of bowls which we have just noted, suggests that the boat inscriptions on bowls show that

such objects belonged to the king's travelling outfit. It would be quite in character with the detailed account keeping, and the strict personal responsibility for things, that each branch of the royal service, for the palace, for travelling, &c., should have its own canteen and furniture.

PL. VIIIA. 1, 2. Pieces of inscriptions of Merpaba.

3. Base of vase inscribed for the "royal palace."

4. Piece of an inscription of king Qa, fitting the piece published in *R. T.* i. viii. 3.

5. Piece with name of king Qa.

6. Piece with a royal name apparently beginning with a bird. Unfortunately, it is so much sand-worn that whether it belongs to a new name cannot be decided.

7. The finest sealing of king Sekhem-ab Perabsen, drawn in seal No. 164, pl. xxi.

8. The jackal standard written in ochre on a piece of an alabaster vase.

9. Part of an inscription, *Neit, her, khent.* Probably of the time of Merneit, by the rough style.

10—12. For adjusting the fragments of stone bowls a frame was employed in order to obtain the forms and draw the restored outlines. This is described in the account of stone bowls, chap. vi.

24. PL. IX. 1. In the tomb of king Khasekhemui were found two pieces of a sceptre (see chamber 48, pl. lxiii.). The larger piece was complete at the thinner end and 23 inches in length; the shorter had been broken from the longer, but was not complete at either end; it was 5 inches long. In the photograph is shown one end of each piece; but it is impossible in a book-plate to represent the whole of such a long slender object on any useful scale. From this plate can be seen the double bands of thick gold which encircle the sceptre at every fourth cylinder, the cylinders of polished sard which form the body, and the corroded rod of copper which binds the whole together. As to the purpose of this object, it

could not be a handle for a fan, as it is too long, and far too liable to fracture of the sard cylinders if any weight bent the copper rod; it is, in fact, only just strong enough to carry its own weight safely. Again, it is complete at the thinner end with a plain cap of gold, which shows no sign of any attachment. It seems clear that it can only have been a ceremonial rod of the king, that is to say, the royal sceptre.

2—10. Six vases of dolomite marble and one vase of carnelian were found together in the tomb of Khasekhemui (near chamber 24, pl. lxiii.). Each of these has a cover of thick gold foil fitted over the top and secured with a double turn of twisted gold wire. Over the tie of the wire a small lump of sealing clay is fixed. With these were two gold bracelets, one perfect, the other crushed by the yielding of the wall.

11. A perfect bowl of diorite was also found covered over by the collapse of one of the walls, between chambers 40 and 44.

12. Pieces of a dish of dolomite marble were found carved in imitation of basket-work.

13—15. Two copper pans, two copper ewers, and a vase of dolomite marble were found together under a collapsed wall opposite chamber 24. One of each kind were grouped together as in fig. 13. The ewers both have double spouts. The motive for so strange a form may be seen perhaps in the co-equal worship of Set and Horus in this reign (see sealings 191—205); the simultaneous offering of libation to both gods could be secured by this double spout. Similarly there is the double co-equal temple of Set and Horus at Kom Ombo, of which the foundation seems likely to belong to this age.

16. A piece of dolomite marble was inserted in a damaged bowl, and held in place by a lining plate, to which it was fastened by long pins of gold. The photograph shows the inner side of the patch with the gold pins projecting.

17—18. Pieces of ivory which seem to have belonged to a carving of a panelled doorway, as they have bands of the usual ornament in relief.

Pl. IXa. 1—3. A dish and two vases of copper were found near together, in the doorway between the south and middle parts of the tomb of Khasekhemui.

4—11. A large mass of funeral models in copper were found stacked together, the tool models inside of the large pan, and the lesser dishes turned over them. The whole group had been covered by a collapsed wall. The models are all roughly cut out of thin sheet copper; they comprise the following forms :—

1 pan, 15 inches across, riveted . fig.	11
1 oval dish, 17 inches long . . „	10
1 „ „ 12 „ „ . . „	10
5 dishes, 9 „ across . . „	6, 7
3 dishes, 6 „ „ (1 broken) „	9
2 tube stands, 10 inches wide (flatted out) . . . . „	8
15 axes, 2 to 5 inches wide . . „	4
16 double harpoons about 4 inches long . . . . . . „	5
16 single harpoons . . . . „	5
12 thick chisels, 2 to 6 inches long . „	5
57 chisels and adzes of thin sheet . „	4
1 dagger of folded sheet . . . „	4
7 chisels „ „ . . . „	4
1 saw . . . . . . „	4
68 needles, pins, &c. (1 with eye) . „	5
3 waste pieces of sheet copper.	

194 model tools, &c., 13 dishes, &c.

From these numbers it seems that the quantities are multiples of 16 ; there being—

8 round dishes.
15 axes (? 1 lost).
16 double harpoons.
16 single harpoons.
64 chisels and adzes of sheet.
68 needles and pins.

It is doubtless from such deposits of models as this group that the many specimens found before have been derived ; and it is fortunate that one complete deposit remained intact to show how such offerings were placed in the tombs. The place of the deposit is marked as "Copper Models," opposite chamber 21 in the plan, pl. lxiii.

Pl. X. See description of Pl. ii. 4 and iiiA. 5.

Pl. XI. See description of Pl. iii. 2 and iiiA. 6.

25. Pl. XII. 1. A piece of a wooden tablet from the tomb of Zer has faintly inscribed on the dusty yellow surface some signs, which show that it had been attached to some offerings for the washing of the king's hands. The vertical shading is in red, the full black parts are in black ink.

2. A fragment of a wooden statuette has traces of the painting in red and black upon it, showing six necklaces, which were probably of spiral gold beads and of stone ball beads. This shows how many strings were worn, even by men, at this period.

3. The upper half of a wooden tablet was so darkened (by oil and smoke ?) that scarcely anything could be discerned. Neither spirit nor benzol would clean it ; but a strong soap lather rubbed hard upon it disclosed gradually the signs here shown. The medium of the inks, both red and black, was so firm that nothing was lost from the signs. This is one of the most valuable pieces recovered, as it shows the free-hand drawing of signs at the finest period of the early kingdom. The firmness and regularity of the lines and the free sweep of the handling are unsurpassed in any writing. It might have been attached to the statuette just noticed, as it seems to name "the standing image of the *ka* of king Zer of the palace *Qed hotep*." The name of the palace is the same as that of king Merpaba (*R.T.* i. vi. 8). The form of the sign *ha* explains the meaning of the small enclosure in the corner ; that is not an inner

chamber as generally supposed, but it is the fortified gateway, as in the Shunet ez Zebib at Abydos, and elsewhere. This was suggested by Maspero in *Proc. Soc. Bib. Arch.* xii. 247.

4. A part of a very thick tablet of ebony shows traces of signs in red and black.

5. A wooden cylinder, found last year near the tomb of Qa, has the remains of the ink-written inscription on it, alternately the shrine of Anpu and the king's name. It was a funerary model of an incised cylinder for sealing.

6. The ivory tablet drawn here is that already mentioned in the account of pl. viii. 3.

CHAPTER IV.

THE SEALINGS AND STELES.

26. PL. XIII. The numbers of the sealings are continuous from those described in *Royal Tombs*, Part I.; thus the number alone suffices to distinguish any published sealing.

89. Only a single impression of the seal of King Ka was found (see pl. ii. 1); but the reality of the name is enforced by the writing of it on the unbaked clay of several jars here figured, and by the ink writing of it on many jars found together in one tomb, which was probably that of king Ka. These latter will be published after being cleaned, but incrustations on them prevent their being yet photographed. The ka arms are turned downward more usually than upward in this name.

90. A small piece of sealing cannot be understood, but it may have some connection with King Ka.

91—92. Several sealings of Narmer were found, which show that Nar alone is the true name, and that *mer* is an epithet separately applied.

93. This seal, of which fragmentary impressions remain, is of Narmer alternating with the word *men*. Were it not for the clear evidence of the ivory tablet from the Naqada-Mena tomb, we should see in this perhaps a reason for Narmer being the name of Mena. There is, however, a possibility that there may have been two kings named Mena, with *ka* names Narmer and Aha. If so, it is nevertheless Aha who is the first king of the Ist Dynasty, because of his position in the roll of eight kings recorded whose tombs can be identified in that order on the ground.

The form of the playing pieces on the *men* sign is exactly that found actually in the tombs (pls. xxxii. 34; xxxv. 5, 6; xli. 74; xlv. 46).

94. A seal with a repetition of lake signs is of the age of Narmer by the associated sealings.

94, 96. Two seals may be either of the time of Mena or a little before that.

97—104. Sealings of King Aha—Mena. Of these 98 and 99 were also found in the Naqada-Mena tomb (*Recherches*, figs. 556, 557); the other six are new, and four found at Naqada are unknown at Abydos. The seal 100 is the only example of the sign *men* that we find in this reign, except that on the back of the wooden tablet, pl. xi. The objects figured on the animal seals are probably traps.

27. 105—107. Sealings of King Zer, with only his name.

108. The most advanced sealing of the early time is the royal seal of King Zer, showing him seated, wearing the crown of Upper and that of Lower Egypt. The work is final as regards the position, the crowns, and the throne; and its type might belong equally to any subsequent age down to Roman times.

109. This seal, with the name of Zer alternating with Zeren and Ta is a valuable link. On a seal of Zet published last year (*R. T.* i. xviii. 2) his name alternates with Ath; which I suggested might refer to Ateth, his name in the list of Sety I. Now we can place together—

Ka name	added	Sety list
ZER	TA	TETA
ZET	ATH	ATETH

From these it seems that we have the original forms of the personal names that were modified by Sety I. Zeren is perhaps a fuller form of the name Zer, as Narmer is a fuller form of Nar.

111 is the latest seal of the prehistoric style with groups of animals; but the *akhu ka* here is an anticipation of the sealings of Merneit and the steles of Den.

112. There are two, or even three, very different styles running on concurrently in the work of these seals. The rough figures of animals and men on a coarse scale come down from the prehistoric time; see 96, 101—104, of Mena, &c.; 111, 113, 114, 122, 123, of Zer; 8, 9, 10, 128, 132, of Zet; after which such disappear. The common hieroglyph seals may rank separately; see 91, 92, 97, 98, 99 of Mena, &c.; 105—107, 116, 124 of Zer; 1—7, 125—127 of Zet. But an entirely different class is that of the very delicate work, which was probably on stone rather than on wood; see 108, 109, 112, 118, 119, 120 of Zer; 135 of Zet. It is not till the time of Den that a general coarse uniformity of style was fixed upon, though even then the royal seal was of the delicate class (pl. vii. 5, 6).

113. See account of stone vase inscription, pl. ii. 15.

114—117. The seals with a shrine should be compared, though none of them are duplicates. On 116 seems to be the earliest form of *sah*. The leopard and bent bars on his back recall the panel of Hesy. The general form of the shrine is like the early huts, with reed sides and interwoven palm rib roof.

123 is the same design as the seal 10 of Zet, but a different seal.

124 is the same design as the seal 20 of Merneit, but differs in having *du* for *zet* in the fortress.

129. The group of four bars in this, as in Nos. 122, 143, is better shown in seal 142, where they are distinguished in two forms.

135. The upper and lower lines are perhaps duplicate in arrangement, the series running *sed nebui* (?); jackal standard; *sekhet nebui; un nebui* (?) *zef; uaz nebui* jackal standard; and another standard, making a six-group seal altogether.

136—163. The sealings of Den are solely of interest for titles and language, and so need not be noticed in this chapter.

28.   164, &c. The sealings from the tomb of Perabsen name in many cases a king Sekhem-ab, and this might have led to difficulties, but for a unique sealing (F.P. coll.), which was found at some site unknown, some years ago, with the form Sekhemperabsen, showing the two names combined.

It will be seen that the hawk of Horus is always over the Sekhem-ab name, while Set is always over the Perabsen name on the seals, as on his stele, pl. xxxi. These are then the Horus and Set names of the king.

The seals of the IInd Dynasty are generally of a smaller style and more elaborate than those of the Ist Dynasty. The sharp detail of those best preserved points to their being made in stone or metal rather than in wood.

The first figures of deities are found on these seals. The hawk-headed god, who has sometimes the feather on the head (No. 199), and the goddess of vegetation (No. 176), with growing plants on her head, and probably the same with lotus sceptre in the hand (Nos. 191, 192, &c.). On the seals of Khasekhemui we see in every case Set and Horus placed together as co-equal. The full-length name of the king expressly refers to this, "the appearing of the dual power in which the two gods are at peace" (see Maspero, *Rév. Crit.*, 15 Dec., 1897).

194. The appearance of the name Amen here is very surprising, but if a more complete impression could be obtained, perhaps it would be explained as Amenti, or otherwise.

210. The impressions of this seal are perhaps the commonest of all; they are entirely on flat

caps of black clay. The name of "the royal mother Hapenmaat " occurs on the tomb of Amten, who made daily offerings in the *ka*-house, or funerary chapel, of this queen (see L. *Denk.* ii. 6). This has been quoted as evidence that she " was queen of one of the last kings of the IIIrd Dynasty," but it only proves that her worship was continued to the end of the IIIrd Dynasty. It seems not improbable that Khasekhemui is the same as Zaza of the list of Sety, last king of the IInd Dynasty (see sect. 6); his queen might well be called the " king-bearer " of Nebka, the founder of the IIIrd Dynasty, and so she might be venerated as the foundress of the IIIrd Dynasty, as Aahmes Nefertari was venerated in the XVIIIth Dynasty. The change from Thinis to Memphis in the title of the IIIrd Dynasty shows a fresh start to have taken place then.

The greater part of the sealings of Khasekhemui are on yellow clay, and very fragmentary, as the area of each originally was only a small part of the whole seal. Hence it is only by comparing dozens of fragments of impressions of each seal that it is possible to reconstruct even the broken views here given.

From the character of the sealings above, it would be clear that Perabsen was intermediate between the Ist Dynasty and Khasekhemui, and this accords with the general features of the tombs.

It is also clear that these two kings cannot long precede King Neterkhet—Zeser of the IIIrd Dynasty, as an impression of a seal of Perabsen was found in his tomb.

I have drawn now all the figures of seals that can possibly be obtained from the thousands of sealings found in our work in the Royal Tombs; and, after going over the collection made in past years, now in the Cairo Museum, I found that only the completion of a few signs could be obtained from that material. Hence it is unlikely that other sealings will add any serious amount to this *corpus*, and also it is unlikely

that sealings will be preserved in less dry localities, such as the temple area. Hence this collection of 216 sealings will be practically all that we shall have for the restoration of the bureaucracy and organization of the first two Dynasties.

29. Pl. XXV. 1, 2 have been already noticed with pls. v. 13 and vA. 6, 4—11. On the bases of stone bowls are occasionally very delicately-drawn signs, which are not hieroglyphic in some cases. Such signs are here shown on enlarged scale. 12 will be noticed with pl. liv.

13—27. Many stone vases bear signs written in ink with a brush. These can scarcely be photographed, owing to the slightness of the ink-stain on dark slate and such stones. Some are shown in *R. T.*, pl. x. Of these 1 = drawing 17, 2 = drawing 21, 3 = drawing 19, 4 is sufficiently clear; 5 = drawing 26, 6 and 7 are sufficiently clear. Only two of these are a king's name, the Setui brushed broadly on slate dishes in figs. 17, 18.

30. Pl. XXVI. The steles drawn here are all shown in photograph in pls. xxviii., xxix., xxixA., xxixB. The numbers are continuous from those published last year, so that it is only needful to quote the number in order to define any of the 146 steles discovered in 1900-1. The forty steles or so, published by M. Amélineau, have no numbers except those added in my outlines of them, *R. T.*, pl. xxxii. It is to be hoped that whenever those are properly published their numbers will begin 147, and so avoid any ambiguity in quotation.

The pieces of the stele of King Zer will be published next year, as unfortunately the photographs of it were lost.

The steles from around the tomb of Zer are mostly so deeply weathered that it is difficult to trace the original relief; see fig. 50, pl. xxviii. In order to draw the outline, or still more, to photograph it, the only method is to fill up all the weathered hollows with sand. Accordingly, handfuls of sand were thrown over each stone, and then the raised figures and signs wiped clear. This was done twice, once for drawing and once for photographing, and hence the drawing is quite an independent interpretation apart from the preparation for photographing. How much is gained in clearness by this sanding is seen by comparing figs. 49, sanded, and 50, the same stone, unsanded. Of course the photographs were taken looking almost vertically downward, the stone being only inclined enough to obtain a shadow to the relief. The drawn outlines were made to scale by using a frame of threads over the stone, and a card ruled in squares beneath the thin drawing-paper. The damages are ignored, the object being to show the best material that can be obtained for reading, while the photograph shows the actual condition. No comparison has yet been made between the photographs and the drawings, which are entirely independent.

It will be noticed that out of 70 stones with signs from around Zer, 16 have names compounded with Neit; one may name Horus (No. 100), but no other deity is mentioned. This strongly shows that the domestics and harem of the king belonged to the Neit worshipping Libyans, rather than to the dynastic race which specially adored Hathor. The relief inscription 59 is duplicated by the inscription 102, written on less than half the size of the other, with red paint on a smooth stone. The differences between the two forms of the signs are instructive.

PL. XXVII. Several of the steles last found were not photographed owing to lack of time caused by illness, but all were drawn, and the drawings of these, together with some of the steles which were too much damaged to be worth photographing, are given in the upper half of this plate. Some had entirely crumbled to flakes since being drawn, owing to the great

rainstorm, and so could not be preserved or photographed.

Besides the Zer steles many were found in finishing the excavations around the tomb of Den. These are drawn in the lower half of pl. xxvii., and photographed in pls. xxx., xxxA. The most interesting of these are the six with uniform titles, 120 to 125, which also occur on No. 21, published last year. It is notable that the king is always named Setui, and never Den, in this title. Two steles had been carefully erased; but by examination in sunshine each sign could be tolerably restored (see Nos. 131, 132).

It may be noted that Nos. 128, 129 seem to contain only a title, as the same occurs on No. 96 with the addition of a name, Ketka.

PL. XXXI. Two steles of king Perabsen were found lying in the sand to the south of his tomb. They seem therefore to have been placed near the entrance to the tomb, which was at the south corner, and not on the east of the tomb, as seems to have been the case in the Ist Dynasty. They are cut in very compact syenite, and much polished by sand wear, so that no sharp edges are left. It was therefore not satisfactory to photograph them in front, by the shadows; and the best result was from the side, by reflections. This makes a rather askew view, which reduces the largest of the two steles to an equality with the lesser. The plate here is an enlargement of a $\frac{1}{4}$-plate snapshot with a hand camera, as it was difficult to fix a stand at the exact angle for the reflections; and I doubt if any better result could have been got by using a stand. The steles are about 5 feet high; cut from natural long waterworn masses of grey syenite; with one face hammer-dressed down to a flat surface, and the hieroglyphs left in relief. The figure of Set above the name has been hammered away in later times.

CHAPTER V.

THE INVENTORY PLATES.

Pls. XXXII.—XLV.

31. In examining a period so little known, and so important, as that of the development of the kingdom, nothing should be slighted; and in even the smallest matters of decoration every fragment should be recorded and added to our knowledge. To describe objects in detail is useless without figures, and therefore a written inventory is merely a tedious legal formality, useless for practical archaeology: and the efficient record is such an outline of every intelligible fragment, that it can be identified in future, can be recognized as joining pieces already known, and can be studied as a whole, comparing one tomb with another. This I have given on the fourteen plates named above: there every object (not given already in photographs) is outlined, or sufficient samples are shown of any large and uniform class, such as the arrow points.

It will be best to notice first such changes as can be traced from tomb to tomb in each class; and then to make some notes on the plates separately.

The bull's-leg supports begin in prehistoric time; one grave at Naqada (No. 3) had a couch supported on bull's legs carved in wood about 15 inches high; they had been entirely eaten by white ants, but yet the form could be traced. The date of this is about S.D. 66 (see *Diospolis Parva* for this mode of dating), or perhaps five or six centuries before the Ist Dynasty. Hence there is a long past in the history of this form, and the use of it in the royal tombs is highly conventional, and remote from its original design. Changes can be seen in the historic time. The use of this form disappears in the reign of Qa, last of the Ist Dynasty, and no such decoration is seen in the tombs of Perabsen and Khasekhemui except one very different fragment in wood (xlv. 6). Yet the idea revived, as it is the constant type of the legs of seats in the Old Kingdom (see *Medum* xiii., L. *Denk.* ii. 10, 84, 85, 86, 109); the lion's legs, however, began to supplant the older form in the latter part of this time (L. *Denk.* ii. 90, 110), and became usual in the XIIth Dynasty (L. *Denk.* ii. 128, 129), and on in the XVIIIth Dynasty (throne of Hatshepsut), and till the Roman time.

Unfortunately most of the perfect examples have been removed to Paris, and their history lost; so it is only from the remains here that we can glean the changes. The wavy line around the leg appears under Mena (xxxii. 9), and continues to Merneit (xxxix. 2), after which it ceases. The number of discs or divisions under the feet decreased as time went on; the maximum in each reign is :—29 under Mena, 19 under Zer, 18 under Merneit, and 14 under Den and Mersekha. The general size diminished, as the largest leg is from Sma (xxxii. 5), and the later ones seem only fit to support caskets and not actual seats.

The arrow points of ivory are common in the earlier part of the Ist Dynasty; but none were found in the tomb of Qa or later. They are often tipped with red ochre, which has been supposed to be a poisoned tip, though iron oxide would be the worst substance to maintain a poison; probably the red colour was put on with the idea of sympathetic magic, in order to draw the arrow to the blood of the animal at which it was shot. The ivory tips were probably all inserted in reeds, like those from a grave near the tomb of Den (pl. viiA. 7); but the ivory has better survived the destruction by man and by insects, so the tips are now nearly all separate. In the tombs of the Mena period and earlier only flint arrow-heads are found (pls. iv., vi.); excepting one specimen of Mena's reign (xxxii. 37). Under Zer the ivory arrow-tip sprang into full use; hundreds were gathered from his tomb; and the variety of forms is greater than in any other reign. Beside the plain circular points (xxxiv. 27—41, many of them with reddened tips), there are the quadrangular barbed tips (42), the pentagonal tips (43), the square tips (44), the oval tips, (45, 46), and the flanged tips (47, 48), beside others of ebony (50, 51). Only the plain circular tips appear in the succeeding reigns, down to Mersekha, except an example of the oval form under Den (xli. 41).

The inlay patterns are scarcely known in the Mena period, the strips with a diagonal cross beginning then (xxxii. 19), and continuing in the time of Zer (xxxiv. 94—99), after which they cease. The twisted cord border begins under Mena (xxxii. 35; iiiA. 1; iv. 16, 17), does not recur till Merneit (xxxix. 37), nor become common till Den (xl. 45—48). The lines beneath the twist are straight at first (xxxii. 35; xl. 46; xli. 30), or curved down (iiiA. 1; iv. 17), but begin to curve up under Den (xli. 32, 35), are straight under Azab (xlii. 72), and curve down under Mersekha (xliii. 41). In the Vth Dynasty (*Deshasheh*, xxvii.), the VIth Dynasty (*Dendereh*, iii.), and in the XIIth Dynasty (L. *Denk.* ii. 130, et seqq.), the lines are curved upward at the ends. The

origin of this pattern is quite unknown; but it mainly appears in representations of the hollows of panelled woodwork. Possibly it represents a plaited cord used to close shutters high up in the panelling, and the lines below are copied from the surplus of the cord resting on the ground.

The pattern of diagonal lines begins under Zer (xxxiv. 53—55), always as a row of squares set diagonally; this becomes cheaper in style under Zet (xxxvii. 46); and though under Den the old style is kept (xl. 56; xli. 42—43), yet very rough imitations occur (xl. 57 —69; xli. 4—6). Such are continued under Azab (xlii. 10, 11, 26, 27, 61—65), Mersekha (xliii. 54, 55), Qa (xliv. 34—37), and even till Khasekhemui (xlv. 29, 32).

Ribbed and mat-work patterns, imitating rush mats and trays, are elaborately wrought in the early work, such as the reed tray of Sma (xxxii. 54), and the mat of bound rushes (62). The mat pattern is on a flat slip of Zer (xxxiv. 92). Plain ribbing occurs under Zet (xxxvii. 56, 62—66). A mat of bound rushes under Merneit (xxxix. 58—61). Plain ribbing (xl. 85—90, 105—106; xli. 48—50) and bound mat-work (xli. 52—54, 65, 69) under Den. The flat mat under Azab (xlii. 68—69). The woven mat of rushes carved in wood under Mersekha (xliii. 27, 28), and plain ribbing (29—33). Plain ribbed ivory inlay, probably from a woven rush mat pattern, under Qa (xliv. 27—31). But in the IInd Dynasty this seems to have disappeared.

Fluted patterns are important as being probably derived from the fluted columns; the earliest is a model column of Zer with sixteen flutings (xxxiv. 73), and a flatter fragment (72). The next is of Den (xl. 107). Under Khasekhemui, an ivory model column with eight lobes, or colonnettes, is seen (xlv. 23), probably also of architectural origin.

Bracelets or bangles are found in most reigns, sometimes abundantly. The flint or chert bangles, made in prehistoric times, continued in use under Mena (xxxii. 42), Zer (xxxv. 60—65), Zet (xxxviii. 45), and even till Perabsen (xlv. 14). The greatest variety of material is under Zer (see pl. xxxv), and after that bracelets are very rare, until many large marble bangles appear in the IInd Dynasty (xlv.).

Cylinder jars of ivory with a wavy line or cord-pattern last until the time of Den (xl. 39); the only surprising variety is that with a row of circles (xxxiv. 71) under Zer, otherwise they closely follow the forms in stone.

Draughtsmen of ivory resemble those figured on the *men* sign (pl. xiii. 93), and are usually about the thickness of a finger or larger (see xxxii. 34; xxxv. 5, 6, 73; xli. 74; xlv. 46). Parts of an alabaster draught-board were found widely scattered in B (xxxii. 71).

32. *Glazed pottery* is first known in the form of beads, very early in the prehistoric time. It occurs here as a bead of Zer (xxxv. 75); as inlay of Zet (xxxvii. 42); as beads (xxxviii. 11, 13, 20, 21, 25, 28, 29, 33); as tile (52), and vases (55, 58); as vases of Den (xxxvii. 78—84, xli. 73, 79, 81); as decoration of Azab (xlii. 75—77); as a vase of Mersekha (xliii. 24, 25; xliv. 10); as beads of Qa (41—43); and as a tall stand, inlays, and beads of Khasekhemui (xlv. 35, 50—62). After such examples and the glaze tile found at Hierakonpolis there can be no hesitation in accepting the date of the IIIrd Dynasty for the doorway of glazed tiles from the step pyramid of Saqqara.

Of metals we find gold, silver, copper, and lead in the prehistoric time, and their uses here in the Ist Dynasty are naturally continuous from that. The gold bar of Mena (iiiA. 7), the gold bracelets of Zer (pl. i.), the gold pin of Zer (vA. 7), the gold frame of Zer (viA. 19), the gold-topped vases, gold bangles, gold-mounted sceptre, and gold pins of Khasekhemui (ix.) have been already described. Of minor objects there are here on pl. xli. a copper rod plated thickly with gold (83), and a knob of thin

gold with a socket and pin-hole to attach it (88); another copper rod plated with gold, and wrought with joints like a reed, is not yet drawn.

Silver is rare in the prehistoric time, and is not found in the Royal Tombs.

Copper wire and nails are usual in many of the tombs (xxxii. 65; xxxviii. 74, 75, 91; xliii. 12, 16). Needles, which we know in early prehistoric use, appear under Zer (xxxv. 84—89), Zet (xxxviii. 76), Den (93, xli. 86), Mersekha (xliii. 13, 14), Qa (xliv. 49), Perabsen (xlv. 18), and Khasekhemui (xlv. 70). Harpoons, with the second fang, unknown in prehistoric copper, were found under Zer (xxxv. 92), and Mersekha (xliv. 12), as well as models under Khasekhemui (ixA. 5).

Small chisels continued to be made from the early prehistoric time, as by Zer (xxxv. 91), Den (xxxviii. 94; xli. 90—93), and Khasekhemui (xlv. 69—75).

Pins like those of the prehistoric age are found under Zer (xxxv. 93—95), Den (xxxviii. 92), Mersekha (xliv. 11), and Qa (48).

The unusual objects are the tweezers (xliii. 15), which are admirably made with a wide hinge and stiff points; the rymer (xliii. 17), the bowl (xliii. 18), the fish-hooks (xlv. 19, 20), and the axe (xlv. 76). For the great mass of copper models see the account of pl. ixA.

33. We will now note the objects on these plates which are outside of the above classes, and which need some explanation.

PL. XXXII. 10, a scratch comb of obsidian, of the type of later prehistoric times. 26—28, model cylinder seals. 38, 40, 42, 43, bone needles. 51, 63, portions of the tops of chair legs. 59, 60, parts of ivory gaming sticks, carved in imitation of slips of reed. 66, dried sycomore figs strung on a thread. 67, 68, a slate palette for grinding eye-paint, with ivory lid to keep dust from it; such were usual (see ii. 11; xxxiv. 23; xxxviii. 2, 50, 51).

PL. XXXIII. An undisturbed tomb was

found by accident in the Osiris temenos last year. The soil was so wet that the bones were mostly dissolved; and only fragments of the skull, crushed under an inverted slate bowl, were preserved. The head had been laid upon a sandstone corn grinder. The beautiful ivory duck dish found by the head was figured last year (*R. T.* i., xxxvii. 1, and see pp. 27, 28, for list of the pottery). Around the sides of the tomb were over two dozen jars of pottery, most of them large. And near the body were sixteen stone vases and bowls, drawn in this pl. xxxiii. Some of the forms, such as 3, 7, 8, are new to us. The strange three-sided pottery bowl, 22, is scarcely known elsewhere, except in stone (see pl. l. 151). A few beads lay by the neck (16—21), with a bit of a shell bangle (23), and a piece of shell scraper (24). A few flint flakes were scattered in the grave (26—35). As there is no museum in England where such a complete tomb can be placed, it was sent to Philadelphia, in order that the whole series should be arranged as originally found. The age of it is certainly close to the reign of Mena, as is seen on comparing the pottery forms *R. T.* i., pls. xxxix., xl., xli., xlii., on which everything from this tomb is marked M.I.

PL. XXXIV. 19, 20. Carved ivory hands from statuettes; compare pl. xxxviii. 54. 21. This portion of a dog is also in pl. viA. 9. 22. This forepart of a dog is like one found by De Morgan in the Naqada Mena-tomb. 56—61. Rods of ivory with flat ends, but longer than these, were found in prehistoric tombs (*Naqada* vii., lxi.). 74. The carving of a bundle of reeds bound together is also in xxxix. 47, and xliii. 35—37. 81. An ivory spoon of the same form as the later prehistoric spoons. 82, 83. An ear of corn, also photographed in pl. vi. 17. 84, 86, 91. Pieces of small bowls of ivory.

PL. XXXV. 2, 3, 4. Portions of boxes of ivory. 7, 9, 10, 15. Parts of the heads of staves or chair legs. 11. Pieces of long conical ivory rod; many such were found, but none fitted together, so it is probable that there were several such rods. 12, 13. Portions of ivory boxes; 13 has a long division down the middle of it; for the inscription see pl. v. 4. 18. Parts of a thin division, such as that in box 13. 20. A hollowed-out base of ivory, drawn on the under side to show the cutting and holes. 24—40. Fragments of ivory bracelets, showing the section, and below it the curvature of the fragment. 41—48. Fragments of decorated bracelets of ivory. 49—52. Fragments of thin bangles of ivory. 53—72. Fragments of bangles of various stones, &c.; the cloudy chalcedony (58) is the most striking of these, being highly polished. 77. A piece of the clear green serpentine which is frequent in prehistoric work. 78—79. Pieces of malachite cut for ornament. 80. A serpent head of lazuli highly polished; this is one of the very few things that might be of uncertain age; and though the snake head (pl. vi. 2) shows that this might occur then, yet its work is so much like that of later times that it may belong to some offering to Osiris. There were a few distinctly late objects found, due to the Osiris worship here, which we do not notice in this volume; but scarcely anything found is of doubtful age. 81. A lazuli plaque shows that other jewellery like that of pl. i. 1 existed here. 83. The overlaying of wood with thin sheet copper was a favourite manufacture; the sheet is usually attached by a close row of very small nails.

PL. XXXVI. Many pieces of wooden throwsticks were found, all of which I compared together, and any possible connections were observed. It is not certain that the pieces in figs. 1, 2, 14, are really connected, but they serve to explain one another. 3—13. Many pieces of wooden wands were found carved in the form of shoots of a reed or rush; nearly all have been burnt, and broken into small pieces. 23, 24, 25. Pieces of unknown objects carved in wood. 27—30. Pieces of thin wood with incised pattern, probably copied from feathers like pl. xliv. 26. 31—34. Pieces of small boxes. 35. Middle plug, of a bow made of two horns. 36. Tip of a horn bow. 39. A curious piece of a wooden cup, which has had a lid dropping in, and secured by twisting it round so that a stud should catch in a slot. 44. Part of a large conical cup of wood.

34. Pl. XXXVII. 19. A wand of wood carved as a human arm, with bracelet; the under side is almost flat. 18, 22. Small studs from boxes. 32. Part of a fluted octagonal column of ivory. 33. Part of an ivory carving of a growing plant. 39, 40. Two fragments of delicate ivory carving of feathers, probably from a royal hawk in ivory of large size. 42. Pieces of glaze for inlaying, of two different designs alike in outline. 57. Piece of wood carved to represent a growing shoot. 59—61. Pieces of ivory tusk pierced with many holes, the purpose of which is unknown. See also pl. xxxix. 55—57.

Pl. XXXVIII. The numbers of the tombs in cemetery W, where the objects were found, are placed below each. 1. Part of a vase of smooth light red pottery, marked with cordage pattern. 2. Part of an ivory lid of a kohl slate. 8. Ivory hair pin, with degraded form of bird on the top: the bird top is common in all the prehistoric periods, see *Diospolis Parva*, p. 21; pl. viв. 378; *Naqada*, lxiii. 47—50; lxiv. 75—84; and this is probably the latest example of it, at the close of the archaic period. 9—29. Examples of the various beads of this age, grouped according to the graves in which they were found. 34. Tip of a wooden staff which has still some of the copper foil covering upon it, and the nails at the side. 34. Piece of inscription on pottery, incised after baking; apparently the same signs as on pl. ii. 15 and pl. xv. 113. 48, 49. Portions of ivory carving of reeds. 50, 51, 53. Small slate palettes for kohl; 50 is much hollowed by use. 54. Finely carved ivory hand from a statuette, see also

pl. xxxiv. 19, 20. 57. A strange piece of inlay, apparently of green glass, partly decomposed, with a dark strip let into it; the form is like that of the piece on pl. xli. 82.

The lower division of plate should have been marked as being from the tomb of Den—Setui. 85. Part of a mace-head of quartz covered with green glaze, like the glazed quartz of Hierakonpolis. 86, 87. Pieces of fluted mace-heads of dolomite marble, as on pl. xli. 95. There is a repeated order of the objects from this tomb, as pls. xxxviii., xxxix. belong to the first season, and pls. xl., xli. to the second season of work. 90. The dried sycomore figs strung together (as on pl. xxxii. 66) were found in great quantities; such strings of figs are commonly sold in Egypt at present.

Pl. XXXIX. 21—25. Pieces of a large serpentine vase (see xli. 94), with cordage pattern carved on it, like the vase of Zer, pl. vi. 27. 26. Pieces of a cylinder vase of ivory, aparently copied from a bucket made of separate staves bound together. 32. Small thin slips of ivory have been found, with a slot running rather more than half through. 34. Fragments of decoration of *uas* and *ankh*, like the bracelet pl. vi. 1. 50. A thick piece of ebony with notched edge, perhaps part of an adjustable rack work. 51. Bull's leg in ebony still attached to the side of a stool or casket. 54. Wooden tablet with ink writing still partly legible.

Pl. XL. 1, 2. Plates of ivory, warped by the burning of the tomb; their purpose is unknown. 10. Parts of a large bodkin of ivory. 21. A fragment of a bone comb, like the prehistoric form (see *Diospolis*, ix. 22, or *Naqada*, lxiv. 70); as this type entirely died out in the later prehistoric age, it seems most probable that this is an older object strayed here. 22. Part of a flat stand of ivory with rope border, and part of the name of Den on the edge. 23. Piece of ivory with the bee from the royal titles. 24. Piece of ivory with part of a *rekhyt* deeply incised. 26. The mouth of a leopard in ivory, front and side view, with drilled holes to be filled with inlay. 28, 29. Pieces of the haunch of a lioness (?). 30—36. Pieces of ivory boxes, &c. 38. Piece of an ivory thistle or corn flower (?). 87. Part of a square of ivory inlay with dovetail on the back, see xliv. 29. 92. Piece of the wig of a life-size figure, which must have been built up of varied material, as this piece is thin. 93. Top of a staff. 96. Horn cut to imitate poles lashed together. 99. Probably part of a rope pattern inlay of different woods.

PL. XLI. 52. A piece of mat-pattern ivory, with signs cut on the edges of the back, to mark the fitting of the next piece. 55. Part of a cylinder of ivory, probably a small case, with recess for fitting in the bottom. 56. Part of a thick cylinder of ivory. 57. Part of an ivory box, with holes for lashing together. 61. Piece of carbonized wood carved with plaited mat pattern. 62. Piece of carbonized wood with relief pattern, apparently of a net with weights hung on it. 70. Piece of wood carved with spiral pattern; it seems to have been coated with copper foil, secured at the row of nail holes along the side. 73, 81. The blue glazed ware is like that found in the previous year, pl. xxxviii. 82, 83. 76. The flat ribbed bead, pierced to serve as a spacer in a necklace or bracelet, shows that such a form was already in use. 77. Fragment of a lioness, like the pieces on pl. xl. 28, 29. 82. Inlay of banded limestone, see pl. xxxviii. 57. 84. Fragment of a model cylinder seal, with ink inscription. 87. Apparently a weight, with a loop top now broken off; as this pattern is well known in the XIXth Dynasty and onward, this may well be later than the tomb.

PL. XLII. Great quantities of ivory inlay from a box were found in the grave X 62. 37. Handle of adze, the only early one yet found. 41. Piece of ink-written tablet of wood. 75-77. Some pieces of narrow ribbed violet glazed ware resemble

those from Zet, Den, and Mersekha; they may have been scattered from one tomb. 78. A piece of an ivory bracelet with a royal name. 83. Block of quartzite sandstone, use unknown.

PL. XLIII. 10. Apparently the two legs of an animal in ivory, from the support of some small object. 21. A highly finished piece of wood carving, of unknown purport. 22. Finely-carved mat-work in wood. 23. Piece of wood with three finger-signs engraved on it. 26. Pieces of wood for inlaying in coarse patterns, probably the middle pieces of the twist pattern, fig. 40, on a large scale. 27, 28. Pieces of a large bier carved with mat pattern; upon such pieces are traces of linen and of silver ornaments which have lain on the bier.

PL. XLIV. 1. Wood carving of a growing shoot of reed. 2. Part of wooden throwstick. 22. Part of another. 23. Piece of horn bracelet. 24. Piece of wood carved with net pattern. 25. Piece of wood carved with a pattern which is inlaid with dark colour. 26. Piece of elaborately-carved feathering from a large figure of a bird in wood; compare the finer ivory carving on pl. xxxvii. 39, 40. The above objects were found in the earth which had been thrown over from the tomb of Qa and mixed with that of Mersekha, so their original place is uncertain. 27—31. Pieces of ivory inlay showing the system of dovetails on the slant, by which each piece could be keyed into a wooden base, without sliding it in a long groove.

PL. XLV. Scarcely anything was found in the tomb of Perabsen, and all these objects have been noted under their classes. The same may be said of the objects from Khasekhemui. While the work of M. Amélineau was going on I bought a copper axe of the same form as fig. 76, but with the numerals "43" upon it.

35. Some analyses of the metals were made by Dr. Gladstone, F.R.S., who has kindly communicated to me the following results.

The alloy of the gold was always with silver,

and in about the same proportions. The samples contained :—

	Zet.	Mersekha.	Qa.
Gold . .	79·7	84·2	84·0
Silver . .	13·4	13·5	12·95
Per cent. .	93·1	97·7	96·95

The loss is probably due to chloride of silver on the surface, which was seen with the microscope. There was no copper or iron. This proportion suggests the native electrum of Asia Minor as the source of the metal.

The copper bands were practically pure copper, but containing about 1 per cent. of manganese. There was no trace of tin.

CHAPTER VI.

THE VASES.

36. When we began to accumulate thousands of fragments of stone vases from the royal tombs, some practical method of dealing with so great a mass of material became urgent. To merely photograph the fragments in front view is absolutely useless for study. In the first place we had to abandon any hope of re-uniting the pieces of broken slate and alabaster. In some of the most promising classes, such as the brims of slate bowls, or the alabaster cylinder jars, we searched exhaustively for possible joinings of the pieces from one tomb, but found so very few that it was clearly hopeless to deal with the less distinctive fragments of bowls without bottom or edge. Hence the slate and alabaster fragments were only searched for such pieces as gave in themselves some distinct form: and the great bulk was left behind on the top surface of our excavations (so as to be accessible if wanted in future) or in heaps at our huts. But every fragment of all other kinds of stone was exhaustively collected: and these tens of thousands of pieces have all been exhaustively compared, so as to secure every possible joining: and nearly all the forms that could be restored have been now drawn, and are given on pls. xlvi. to liiiG. Most unfortunately for science much had been already carried away to Paris, and has lain there since, entirely useless and unstudied. Whenever that mass of fragments is open to research it is obvious that most of them will fall into place along with the other pieces, which I have already classified into hundreds of separate bowls. At present any such re-union of fragments is declined. So the only course now is to publish the forms which I have restored.

37. How to separate and identify the varied forms from each cart-load of broken scraps, was the problem. In the first place all the pieces from any one tomb were kept together, and such were treated without reference to any other tomb until worked up. They were sorted into about two dozen different classes of materials, such as quartz crystal, basalt, porphyry, syenite, granite, volcanic ash, metamorphic, serpentine, slate, dolomite marble, alabaster, various coloured marbles and limestones, saccharine marble, grey limestone, and coarse white limestone. The classes were made as small as was compatible with no piece being of uncertain class.

All the pieces of one class from one tomb were then laid out, often numbering many hundreds; such as were of any peculiar stone were put together, and the rest were laid with all the brims together in lines along the top of the table, all the middle pieces laid with the axis vertical, and all bases together along the lower edge of the table. A piece of brim was then compared with every other piece, and any of the same radius of curvature and profile were put together. The same was done with the bases. The brims and bases thus sorted were then compared with the middle pieces, especially noting the angle of the line of fracture with the vertical, which gives the quickest means of identification. Sometimes several different bowls were so nearly alike that only a complete and exhaustive trial of fitting each piece to every other would suffice to settle their real connection. Such work is tedious and exhausts the attention, so that it cannot be usefully continued for long; and difficult tables-full would sometimes remain for many days, being attacked by different sorters whenever other work allowed.

The final condition of all these fragments now is that there are some eight hundred paper packets each containing the fragments of some one vase, each labelled with the name of the material, the tomb, and the number of the form. Whenever fresh fragments may be available, it is only needful to look over the forms drawn, for any that correspond, in order to at once turn up the parcels of those forms, and see if a joining is possible. In this way, after I had done the greater part of our material, I frequently identified the rest of a vase from a single fragment in a minute or two.

38. The restoration of the forms from the fragments was another question. Any piece of brim, or of base edge, gives two facts, (1) the radius of curvature, or distance from the axis of the vase, and (2) the angle that the side makes with the horizontal. Hence it is possible to place a piece of brim and a piece of base into approximate position without any intermediate parts or joining. The mode of doing this may be seen at the base of pl. viiiA. A frame, like three sides of a cube, has on the floor of it a card ruled into circles, half an inch apart. A piece of brim is set on this, mouth down, rocked until the edge rests fairly on the card all along, and, if needful, held at that angle by a leg of wax stuck on to it. Then it is slid to and from the centre until it fits parallel to the nearest circles. Thus it is put at the right angle, and centred on the card. Next the piece of base has its curvature measured by a celluloid film ruled with circles. And it is then stuck with wax on to the foot of a sliding rod centred to the axis, the rod moving in grooves exactly above the centre of the card. Thus the piece of base can be slid up and down on the same axis as that of

the piece of brim; and if the pieces extend to the same radius of the bowl, they are merely adjusted to bring the outer surfaces into one line; or if there is an interval, yet it can be easily seen, within a very small amount, what the height must be to render their outlines into one curve.

For the drawings the following measurements were taken: Height; radius, maximum; radius of lip; radius of base; height of maximum radius; angle of rise from base; if needful, angle of side with brim; sometimes also the angle at some intermediate point of the curve, or the height and radius of points along the curve, especially for pieces of large bowls. After marking all these dimensions and angles on half scale, a freehand outline was drawn, looking closely at the character of the form. Then the thickness of the bowl was measured at two or three points, and the inside curve was drawn. Lastly the drawings were all inked in by Miss Orme, blacking the whole of the ground, and drawing the inner curve. For dark materials this drawing is then photographically reversed, so as to give a dark figure with a white line. The numbers and references were written in with white on the black ground. The forms are all classified from the most open to the most closed.

39. Pls. xlvi., xlvii. QUARTZ CRYSTAL. These vases were mostly of smaller size than those in other materials. The colour varies a good deal, and serves to distinguish the vases into several classes. The *chatoyant* quartz, often with opal tints in the sunshine, was used mainly for thick forms, and is restricted to Den. The clear yellowish or smoky quartz was mainly of small size, and used by Qa. The very thin, clear quartz, like a watch-glass, belongs to Mersekha. The fragments of No. 22 were scattered in three tombs; but they probably belong together, as it is a peculiar oval bowl, of which the two sections are shown, one inside the other. The piece of base is intermediate between the two

axes. Where an inner curve is not continuous in these restorations, it means that there are no fragments completing the whole outline, but that it is carried out by projection from the pieces at top and base. Where either top or base is entirely missing, then a broken outline is left, as in Nos. 3, 5, 6, 10, 13, 14, &c. ; 46 is probably the neck of a small bottle.

The thick salt-cellar forms, Nos. 48—50, are only found in crystal.

Pls. xlvi. A, B. BASALT. The brown basalt is of the same quality as that used in the fourth dynasty for building, coming from El Khankah near Bubastis. It is too soft to bear working very thin in general, and most of the vases are thick and heavy. The tall cylinder vases, with wavy or rope lines (Nos. 76—83) are seldom found except in basalt and alabaster. Most of the other basalt forms also are akin to those in limestone and alabaster, all three materials belonging to the Nile valley ; while the forms of the materials from the igneous rocks of the eastern desert, are of a different class.

Pls. xlviii. A, B, xlix. PORPHYRY AND SYENITE. There are here classed together some very different materials, but they vary so imperceptibly one from another that it is impossible to make a clear division. The general nature of each vase is shown by *sy.* for syenite, where the felspar surrounds the darker base ; *por.* for porphyry, where the darker base surrounds the felspar crystals, *large por.* for large grained porphyry, with detached big crystals of felspar, and *di.* for diorite, meaning the rather soapy-looking, speckled, translucent, sub-crystalline rock. Probably a petrologist would replace each of these names by much longer, less known, and more exact terms ; but my object is to distinguish the rocks by the obvious appearances which the ancients probably recognized. The fluted bowl of red porphyry, No. 88, is like some pieces found at Naqada, which were probably of the same age. The pink granite, No. 102, was published last year in *R. T.* i. vi. 8.

The large jars, Nos. 122 –127, are only found otherwise in serpentine ; they descend from the types which were usual throughout the latter half of the prehistoric age. The flattened ovoid forms, Nos. 129-132, also have as long a history of descent from the prehistoric. The fluted form, 129, is of the same class as the fluted bowl, 88, from the pattern of the base it is evidently copied from basket work. The same type was in the Naqada Mena-tomb (De Morgan, *Recherches*, ii. fig. 684). The very large porphyry with a dark grey base, like 133, seems to have been only worked in the age of Mena, as the examples all came from group B, and are like others in the Naqada Mena-tomb (*Rech.* ii. fig. 603).

Pls. xlixA., l., lA., li. VOLCANIC. The variety of the volcanic material is very difficult to classify. I have distinguished in the drawings between *volc.* which includes all material of varying grain such as volcanic ash, crystalline lavas, &c. ; and *met.* (metamorphic), which includes all materials which have a uniform fine grain of recrystallization or is clearly much altered. As all metamorphic rocks are included here, gneiss has to be in this class. It was needful to wet most of the pieces and examine with a magnifier before even this rough classification could be made. The three-lobed bowl, No. 151, is very unusual ; the same idea occurs in pottery of the age of Mena (pl. xxxiii. 22).

Pl. liA. SERPENTINE. The colour of this varies greatly ; some is of the green translucent kind usual in the prehistoric age ; other is green with red veins : other is brown ; and the large jars are coarse yellow with black veins much decomposed.

40. Pl. liB. SLATE. The hundreds of slate bowls are nearly all of the types 222—227. One bowl, 214, is oval, the drawing showing the narrow view, and the wide view being about half as wide again. Two curious necked vases occur, 228, 229. And besides the cylinder

vase, 230, there is another in the photographs, pl. viiA. 16.

Pls. liC., D, E. DOLOMITE MARBLE. This material varies much, but cannot be confounded with any other class. It is hard, opaque, white, with veins: sometimes the veining is of clearer white, but usually of grey, and sometimes of quartz almost black. The magnesia of the dolomite is left on the surface as a powdery white incrustation, if it has been exposed to solution by weathering. The forms are much like those of the volcanic vases. The spout in No. 265 is also met with in volcanic ash from other sites. The type No. 281 is a favourite in the earlier tombs; it is often of a pinky white colour, and scarcely at all veined. The form 288 is a plain ring of stone, perhaps an armlet.

Pls. liF., G, H, lii., liii., liiiA. ALABASTER. This is the commonest material of all, and is mainly used for cylinder jars, which are of all sizes up to nine inches across. The bowls, which are also very common, are not fully represented here, as illness during the last week at Abydos prevented my working over a large quantity. The flat saucers, Nos. 295—298, are like what were found at Hierakonpolis, probably of the age of Narmer (*Hierakon.* pl. xxxiv.). The cylinder jars are divided into those without a band (336—344), with wavy band (345—355), with rope band (356—392), and with plain band (393—398); and in each of these classes the examples are put in historical order. The wavy band belongs to the earlier part of this age, and disappears altogether half-way through the Ist Dynasty. The most important example of the rope band is the great vase of Narmer, No. 359. The rope pattern is often made with wide cuts across the ridge at all periods of this age. The double band (368, 369) is very unusual. Some examples are only given in half view (381—388), to save space; but paired thus they give the general effect of the size. The very narrow forms, 379, 392, belong to the

later time. This type had begun early in the prehistoric (*Diospolis*, iii.); it lasted on to the VIth Dynasty, widened much to the top with flat brim (*Dios.* xxviii.); in the Xth Dynasty it became more cylindrical again (*Dios.* xxviii.); and in the XIIth Dynasty it again widened much to the top (*Dios.* xxix.); after which it seems to have become extinct.

Pls. liiiB., C, D. COLOURED LIMESTONE. A great variety of marbles, limestones, and breccias are all grouped together here, as being similar in nature, and none of them numerous enough to form a separate class. They are more usual in the later reigns, as soft stone supplanted the hard igneous rocks that were most used at first. The forms are not distinctive; but some unusual types occur, such as 403-6, 412, 454, and the old prehistoric form 455, which comes to its end in this dynasty. The pendant form of this type differs much from the spheroidal type given in Nos. 129—131: so far as I have seen the examples, both from the royal tombs and elsewhere, the pendant form was only made in breccia, and in a late period; the spheroidal form was the earlier, and was preferred always for the hard rocks.

Pls. liiiE., F. GREY LIMESTONE. There are some varieties in this class; the grey and white saccharine marble, often with green tints; the brown-grey limestone taking a soapy polish; the grey and white shelly limestone; the dull earthy limestone; and soft grey taking a high polish. The forms are mostly usual types; but the little ribbed saucer, 462, is unique; and the oval jar with wavy handle, 483, differs from all other examples.

Pl. liiiG. ROUGH LIMESTONE. This class is always coarse and thick in the forms, the material being unsuited to the finer work; and most of it is of the later period.

41. Beside the vase forms directly drawn here there were many examples which were so closely like others already drawn that it was needless to repeat them. They need, however,

to be recorded in order to be able to identify any fragments that may be elsewhere, and to show what are the forms known in each material. Also the statistics of the use of materials in different reigns, and the history of the different types, will require a complete record such as this, whenever they are worked out. In the following lists the materials are classed as in the plates, the number of the form duplicated is given, the tomb letter, and any needful detail of the material, or note of different size.

Crystal.

- 7 U.W
- 14 P $\frac{3}{4}$
- 33 U thin
- U $\frac{2}{1}$
- 34 T
- Y
- 37 T 8 high
- 38 T lesser
- 39 P
- 41 U
- 43 $\frac{1}{2}$, thin

Basalt.

- 81 B
- 150 X frag.
- 152 Q
- 229 Y 5 thick
- 299 O brim
- 310 X frag.
- 411 T lesser

Serpentine.

- 109 B
- 121 T lesser
- 143 Q yell. bk.
- 150 O
- 184 T grey
- 195 O gn. vein
- 262 O $\frac{1}{2}$
- 281 O transp.
- 446 T lesser
- 474 O gn. $\frac{2}{3}$

Syenite, &c.

- 91 T sy. por.
- 92 B sy.
- 103 Y 8 sy.
- 109 O flatter
- 118 T gneiss $\frac{3}{2}$
- 129 Q bk. wt. por.
- 129 T bk. wt. sy.
- 147 B sy. thick
- 148 U diorite
- 156 Q por.
- 176 Y sy.
- 176 Q diorite
- 181 O sy. $\frac{3}{4}$
- 217 T por.
- 233 B por.
- 237 O sy.
- 240 B por.
- 259 Y sy.
- 268 Y sy.
- 269 Y sy.
- 411 Z sy.
- 446 T diorite
- 452 Y por.
- 469 Z sy.
- 497 P sy.

Volcanic, &c.

- 94 T volc.
- 94 T gn. met.
- 113 U met.
- 119 T met.
- 119 Y gneiss
- 119 Q gneiss
- 150 Q gy. met.
- 166 O met.
- 166 O met.
- 170 T volc.
- 177 T met.
- 179 T volc.
- 179 Q volc. $\frac{3}{4}$
- 180 Q volc.
- 184 Y met.
- 212 T met.
- 213 T met.
- 268 T met.
- 270 Y met.
- 418 O volc.
- 466 T met.
- 471 T met.
- 474 T met.
- 477 T volc. $\frac{3}{4}$
- 478 T volc.
- 481 O volc.
- 493 T met.

Slate.

- 62 O thin
- 86 T $\frac{4}{3}$
- 94 X burnt
- 104 O
- 138 UQ
- 145 T thick
- 149 Q
- 150 T
- 156 O lesser
- 172 T $\frac{4}{3}$
- 185 T
- 195 O
- 207 T $\frac{2}{3}$
- 217 T
- 226 Z
- 240 T
- 240 Z
- 252 O $\frac{3}{2}$
- 257 T
- 262 T
- 267 O
- 268 B
- 323 T (two)
- 434 O thin
- 434 T
- 436 T $\frac{3}{2}$
- 443 O
- 443 T
- 449 T
- 452 O $\frac{5}{6}$
- 485 UQ
- 496 T thinner

Dolomite Marble.

- 60 T $\frac{3}{4}$
- 61 Q
- 83 T
- 101 O
- 109 T $\frac{3}{4}$
- 116 T $\frac{3}{4}$
- 119 X
- 149 Q
- 176 T
- 179 T
- 179 B 11
- 179 Y
- 183 T
- 184 Q
- 184 Y
- 193 O $\frac{3}{4}$
- 195 O $\frac{1}{2}$
- 220 Y $\frac{2}{3}$
- 240 U
- 243 Q
- 246 O
- 246 T
- 248 O $\frac{1}{2}$
- 260 Q
- 262 O
- 262 Z
- 267 Y
- 268 T
- 277 O
- 277 T
- 280 X.Y.Z.
- 281 O
- 281 T
- 287 X
- 309 T $\frac{2}{3}$
- 327 T $\frac{2}{3}$
- 416 U
- 443 T
- 443 P
- 444 Z
- 448 O
- 459 B 10
- 460 O
- 481 P

Alabaster.

- 38 Y
- 60 O $\frac{3}{4}$
- 60 O $\frac{4}{5}$
- 61 Y
- 62 U
- 81 B 15
- 109 Z
- 113 U
- 134 U
- 147 X
- 177 U $\frac{4}{3}$
- 213 U gyps.
- 217 O
- 233 Z
- 233 Y
- 236 X
- 275 Z
- 281 O four.
- 293 X
- 299 O
- 321 Z
- 323 Z
- 365 O $\frac{2}{3}$
- 383 B
- 411 O gyps.
- 425 Z calc.
- 428 U
- 448 U
- 468 T

Coloured Limestone.

- 60 O breccia $\frac{4}{5}$
- 82 T pink
- 86 T red
- 100 O pink
- 103 B 15 breccia $\frac{3}{2}$ thick
- 129 U breccia
- 149 X 56 pink
- 164 O pink $\frac{3}{2}$
- 167 T buff
- 176 U pink
- 183 T pink wt.
- 199 Y breccia
- 217 T creamy
- 217 T pink $\frac{4}{3}$
- 217 X breccia
- 233 T pink
- 255 X breccia
- 262 O pink wt. $\frac{1}{2}$
- 281 O pinky
- 281 O red
- 281 W pinky
- 326 X breccia
- 401 O red wt. $\frac{2}{3}$
- 418 O pink $\frac{4}{3}$
- 418 O pink $\frac{2}{3}$
- 425 X breccia
- 429 U pink
- 429 X creamy
- 433 O buff purp.
- 434 O breccia $\frac{1}{2}$
- 437 X pink
- 449 T buff br.
- 452 X breccia
- 464 O red bl.
- 466 Q red
- 466 X creamy
- 496 Q breccia
- 497 T breccia

Grey Limestone.

- 38 UQ lenticular
- 181 T shelly
- 185 T shelly
- 253 Q hard
- 253 T veined $\frac{3}{4}$
- 260 UQ
- 262 T veined
- 287 B hard
- 287 Z
- 448 U saccharine
- 475 Q gy. and gn. saccharine
- 476 T banded gy. wt.
- 481 T cloudy
- 483 T hard

Rough Limestone.

- 62 O $\frac{4}{5}$
- 99 O
- 106 B thick
- 144 T
- 149 Q
- 150 O $\frac{4}{3}$
- 195 O
- 244 O
- 246 Y
- 246 Q
- 309 Q
- 429 Q creamy
- 447 T
- 457 O
- 496 Q nummulitic.

42. Last year many pieces of pottery closely resembling the Aegean ware came to light in the tomb of Mersekha, and a few in that of Den : these are shown on pl. liv. Before publishing these I thought best to ascertain whether such pottery was already known in any other connection, and if it were possibly due to any later offerings than those of the Ist Dynasty. The opinion of Prof. Furt-wängler and Prof. Wolters was that the ware most resembled the earliest Island pottery ; but that the exact fabric was yet unfixed on Greek soil. Mr. Arthur Evans, however, claims that it resembles some of the pottery of the IInd Dynasty from El Kab, which I have not yet had the opportunity of comparing with it. If so, it would only show that such pottery continued to come from the same source, wherever that might have been. We will now look at the internal and external evidences.

The body of the ware is identical with that of later Aegean or Mykenaean pottery ; the same soft, light-brown clay, decomposing in flakes. Such is quite unknown in Egypt. The face is finished with a finer clay, in a manner unknown in Egypt until the Greek influence of the XVIIIth Dynasty. The colouring is the iron oxide, burnt either red or black, exactly as on all the Mykenaean pottery ; a colouring unknown in Egypt until the Greek influence, and then very unusual. The patterns are those common on the Mykenaean pottery, such as < < < <, spot patterns, and zigzag lines : all of these are unknown in Egyptian work, and indeed no patterned Egyptian pottery is known until the XVIIIth Dynasty.

With these is also another class of pottery (at the base of the plate) which is entirely un-Egyptian in the forms, the colour, and the paste. The outlines of it are clearly of the European family, and never occur in Egypt until copied in a late time. The three small handles only appear in the XIXth Dynasty, when Greek influence and pottery became common. The marks on the pottery are not Egyptian ; another example of such found this year is shown on pl. xxv. 12.

The external evidence for the decorated pottery is that the fragments are nearly all found in the ruins of one tomb—that of Mersekha ; and no later offerings were placed there beyond a small sprinkle of little saucers of the XXIInd Dynasty. Whereas, in contrast, not a single piece is found on the tomb of Zer, —the Osiris shrine—where tons of pottery offerings were placed from the XVIIIth to the XXVIth Dynasties. The evidence is strong that it was not then brought with later offerings. Again, the few bits found in the earlier tomb of Den (the first three pieces on the plate and others this year) are of a ruder and less complete fabric, and might well precede the rest by a few generations.

The evidence about the second class, the unpainted pottery, is now absolute. In the small N.-W. cell of the tomb of Zer some offerings remained unmoved, owing to the later brick stair having been built over them in the XVIIIth Dynasty, after the burning of the tomb. In this cell was an important group of pottery, caked together by resins and burnt linen in the burning of the tomb. This pottery is of the European class, of forms quite unknown in Egypt, and clearly the same fabric as the pottery at the base of pl. liv. Unfortunately my illness at the last prevented my drawing or photographing it for this volume ; so it will be published next year. Suffice to say here that pottery of a fabric and of forms entirely foreign to Egypt, and of European character, is now absolutely dated to the second king of the Ist Dynasty, about 4700 B.C.

What difficulty is there in accepting the good evidence here given for the beginning of such Aegean pottery ? We now know that in Crete a grand civilization was in full course before 2000 B.C. ; and was in communication with Egypt, as shown by the diorite statue of the

XIIth Dynasty and the jar lid of King Khyan. That such a civilization had a long past and growth, cannot be doubted. Many earlier stages of it are found, town below town exists beneath the palace of Knossos; and that men were beginning to make the characteristic painted pottery in the Aegean at 4700 B.C. is a perfectly open question on the Greek side. When the only evidences of age in Crete pledge us to go back from classical times full half-way to the Egyptian date, and then show that we are very far from the beginning, it seems that we should be led in any case by the Greek evidence to within some few centuries of the age here indicated. And there is absolutely nothing to cut short the scale of the earliest ages in Greece. The only conclusion possible, until some equally clear evidence may appear to contradict this, is to accept the dating of the rise of decorated pottery in the Aegean to 4700 B.C.

43. The Marks on pottery, pls. lv., A B C D, are of the same classes as those described last year. It is only by completely collecting these, and publishing them year by year, that it will be possible at last to build up a history of the use of such signs, and to disentangle the hieroglyphic from the linear signs. That the latter go back to early prehistoric time is certain; and that they continued in use until the alphabets of the Mediterranean were selected from them, is shown by the tables published in the last volume (*Royal Tombs*, i. p. 32).

In the last volume the part of a name, No. 1 (on pl. xliv.), which is the tail of a fish, we can now place as belonging to Narmer, since we find the fish alone in the square on his sealings.

The names of king Ka, which are the most important of the incised marks, are given on pl. xiii. in this volume, for comparison with his seal.

The groups, pl. lv., 6 to 13, are probably all blundered examples of Mersekha. Nos. 16—26 are the *sa-ha* palace name; not distinguished between *sa-ha-neb*, *sa-ha-ka*, and *sa-*

ha- . . . , the palaces of the end of the Ist and beginning of the IInd Dynasty.

27—48 give the *Ka* arms, often connected with other signs.

49—66 show some animal, probably the same as on stele. 64 (pl. xxix.), which may be the jerboa.

67—77 are birds, but cannot be distinguished, as the different forms were not well fixed by this time.

78—94 are serpents; the group of two serpents being usual.

95—102 are fishes.

103—135 show a form which may be intended for the winged disc; *neter ka* is often placed with it, and also the yoke sign.

136—153 are all the *neter* sign in various combinations.

154—163 are the hill signs, both three and two hills.

165 is the hieroglyph *th*.

166 is the hieroglyph *mer*, the hoe.

168—171 show the hieroglyph *hotep*.

172—174 the *sa* hieroglyph.

176—178 give the so-called yoke sign, for which see sealings 115, 116, on pl. xvi.

179—187 the plant sign, *res*, " southern."

188—195 the star and crescent, or star in a circle.

198—204 the divided square, perhaps the mat hieroglyph *p*.

206 the group *sennu* in hieroglyphs.

228—230 the double vase.

231, 232 the spout vase.

233—240 the *ankh* sign.

242—293 the dagger *tep* sign; combined with the *Ka* arms, a bird, the *neter* sign, a spotted disc, &c.

The groups of signs after this, 294—491, are not such as can be identified with any hieroglyphs, but mostly belong to the system of linear signs which is already classified in the previous volume. Plates lvi., lviA., and lvii. have been noticed in detail in the descriptions of the tombs.

CHAPTER VII.

THE INSCRIPTIONS.

By F. Ll. Griffith, M.A., F.S.A.

44. The second campaign at Abydos has again doubled the mass of known inscriptions belonging to the period of the earliest dynasties. This time there are few inscriptions on vases, but in other classes more material has been recovered than was the case even last year. Besides objects dating from the compact group of First Dynasty kings following Mena, which formed the bulk of the finds in 1899-1900, there are this year others, both earlier and later. General progress and development is observable from the kings before Mena, through the First Dynasty and the Second Dynasty, towards the methods, mannerisms, expressions, and titles current in the Fourth and later Dynasties. But in the new finds there is not much that strikes one as wholly novel and unrepresented in those of last year, and it is disappointing that there is no single inscription so extensive even as the fine stele of Sabef: a series of such monuments would have cleared up a multitude of difficulties. In the matter of inscription, therefore, this year's work is rather calculated to solidify the results of last year than to start fresh lines of discovery. Notwithstanding the large quantity of new material, progress in the reading of these very archaic inscriptions is likely to be slow. The titles of the kings and some titles of officials can be recognized easily by analogous groups used later with the same meaning; some proper names also are fairly obvious; but the interpretation of the rest is almost without exception so impossible or so hazardous, that one is unwilling to venture a guess as to the meaning. The legends, besides being excessively concise, are in many cases very ill-engraved, and the individual signs composing them are uncertain; to their general sense we have but vague clues, the abundant remains of later times offering no parallels to the tablet inscriptions and sealings. Professor Petrie's second instalment of material follows so quickly on the first that no criticism of the readings proposed in Part I. has yet found its way into print. Such criticism is certain to be forthcoming before long, and cannot fail to be beneficial. Meanwhile, in my brief examination of the plates of inscriptions, I have the advantage of perusing Mr. Petrie's descriptions, with notes of parallel inscriptions and conjectures as to the meaning of the legends; as also a conspectus of the titles, etc., found on the jar-sealings. The latter was quickly drawn up at Mr. Petrie's request by Mr. Herbert Thompson, who has annotated it with references to titles of the later Old Kingdom and has handed it to me to make use of in this chapter. I have drawn largely from both, and in most cases without special acknowledgment. There is doubtless much more to be said on the subject of these inscriptions, but there is no time for research and verification.

45. Pl. ii. 1. Apparently a Horus-name ⊔; see Pl. xiii. 1, where the Horus-stand seems clear, and the hands are turned downwards ⊓.

8—11. The principal sign here is probably ⊻ s'm or sm' (hardly ⌇). The group ⊻ is paralleled by ⌣ and ⌣ in R. T., i., Pl. iv. 3, xxxii. 32. According to these Sma is probably a royal name: otherwise one would be inclined to translate Sm'(·t) Nb·ty, "consort of the Double Dominion," especially in No. 11, where the name Neithotep is added, compare v. 13, 14 and xxv. 1. No. 10 is fractured above the ⊻.

13, 14 seem to read ⌇🦅, suggesting the name of the goddess Bast (more precisely written

Ubastet, as Prof. Spiegelberg has recently pointed out); but in *R. T.*, i., Pl. iv. 5, and below v.A, figs. 6, 22, 23, xxv. 2 we have [glyph]. These names may very plausibly be rendered "Soul of Isis" and "brow (or horns) of Isis"; but they are of course open to other interpretations.

15 offers a very clear instance of the group [glyphs] Rekhyt, preceded perhaps by the [glyph] of Pl. xv., No. 113, and Pl. xxxviii. 35.

Pl. iii. 1. The palm-tree [glyph] is a rare sign in ordinary hieroglyphic; as Mr. Thompson has remarked to me, the group here (no doubt a proper name) probably corresponds to the later [glyph] *y'm-yb* "Grace of heart."

2. Note [glyph] without projections at the top, also in 4 and iii.A 5, 6 = x. 2 and xi. 2, *R. T.*, i., Pl. xiv. 12.

4, 6. Note [glyph] in what seems to be its usual form in the Old Kingdom, and the signs for the South and North countries. One might conjecture that it means "Receiving the princes of the North and South," or "receiving the Kingdom of the North and South." Behind [glyph] is the palace gate-tower [glyph], and beyond is [glyph] above [glyph] or [glyph] Horus (?), and [glyph] the symbol of [glyphs], Anubis the embalmer (?).

8. Mr. Petrie reads behind the ibex-head [glyphs]

Pl. iii.A 5, 6 = x. 2, xi. 2.

46. Pl. v. The variations of the sign forming the king's name are considerable, but they point very clearly to its identity with the printed [glyph] *zer*, a bundle of stems (?) tied together. For forms of [glyph] dating from the Vth Dynasty see *Ptahhetep*, I., Pl. xiv. 314, 321. The best examples here are in Pl. v., figs. 4, 7 (two ties); on the seals in Pl. xv. there is only one tie, as in the normal forms.

1. This inscription is remarkable for the vertical division-line between two inscriptions which face in opposite ways, exactly as in later times. [glyph] looks like a city-name. Possibly [glyph] is suppressed, as may be expected to happen sometimes, in which case we should have [glyph] or Mendes; but as yet no firm ground can be reached in regard to geographical names of this period. The animal might be a goat or a *tragelaphus* sheep (as at Mendes), but is much more like a cow, with an ostrich feather between its horns. The sign below is [glyph] rather than [glyph]. Compare with this Pl. vi.A 2.

2. The enclosure contains [glyphs].

3. Compare [glyphs] *ht š Ḥrw* (?) in *R. T.*, i., Pl. xvii. 28.

13, 14. [glyph] which Mr. Petrie reads "washing of the hand of the Double Lord," reminds one of *R. T.*, i., Pl. xxxii., fig. 32, and above Pl. ii., fig. 8.

Pl. v.A. 13. Compare Pl. vii.A 2. The enclosure contains apparently three bound captives.

6, 22, 23. Compare above Pl. ii., fig. 13.

Pl. vi.A. 4. [glyphs]

24. [glyphs]. A connection between the word *št* and the jackal is shown by the hieroglyph [glyph].

47. Pl. vii. 5, 6. The signs on this important seal seem from the photograph to be—

[glyphs]

With regard to the royal name [glyph], W. Max Müller, who would read it Khasty (*Ḥ's·ty*), has ingeniously suggested that, being in hieratic, and especially in late times in linear hieroglyphic, written [glyph], it was then misread *Qnqn*, producing Manetho's Kenkenes.

7. Prof. Sayce has suggested that in this remarkable inscription [glyph] is only another way of writing [glyph]. The figure in front is very interesting. It is a very fine example of the symbol of the rare divinity Mafdet. It is

E

found again *R. T.*, i., Pl. xxxii. 39, apparently in connection with hunting, and by uniting fig. 10 on the present plate[1] with fig. 4 of *R. T.*, i., Pl. vii., we obtain a figure of the animal apparently holding ⎛ and with the name written ⸻. The spelling Mafdet in the Pyramid Texts shows that ⸻ is here to have its full word-sign value ⸻. The form of the name *M'-f d·t*, with the masculine suffix *f*, suggests that the divinity is male; but the composition of the name is not certain, and the animal resembles a lioness, and could hardly be a leopard, as there is no indication of spots. Probably, therefore, Mafdet is a goddess. In the *Book of the Dead* (see *Hieroglyphs*, p. 62, where references are given), in texts of the New Kingdom, the name is determined by a cat. In the Pyramid Texts it is followed by ⸻; in fig. 7, etc., as on the Palermo stone, the lioness is figured as if it were walking up the sign ⸻. The latter (see *Hieroglyphs* and *Ptahhetep*, I.) is difficult to explain, but in the present instance we have a very fine example. From this we see that it consists of a tapering rod or stick, curved over into a rather broad hook at the top, and a handled knife-blade, which is strongly lashed to the rod beneath the hook, and points outwards and slightly upwards on the same side. It scarcely seems to be an instrument for use, but rather a ceremonial combination of the instruments for catching (hooked stick), for binding (thongs or cords), and for killing (knife), whether in regard to malefactors or to animals. It would thus be very appropriate as a symbol of "attendants" armed to follow their lord in the execution of justice, in war, or in the chase; and of the feline goddess of hunting and of vengeance: compare the *fasces* of the lictors. M. Capart has quoted some of the highly symbolic representations in the

tombs of the kings, in which a human head is depicted dangling from the hooked staff of ⸻. This points to the same interpretation. Further we may note that in *R. T.*, i., Pl. xxxii. 39, the feline symbol of Mafdet and the jackal symbol of Anubis or of Upuat (Ophoïs) are seen associated. I think that it may be affirmed that the jackal was the servant messenger and attendant of the gods; and probably Mafdet likewise accompanied them as the fierce hunter and executioner in their employ.

8. Note that the shrine surmounted by a bucranium, as here shown, forms the hieroglyphic name of Crocodilopolis, the capital of the Faiyum, and is read ⸻, Shedet.

10. See note on 7.

11. Compare the closely similar fragment *R. T.*, i., Pl. xi. 4 = xv. 18. It shows that the explanation suggested for that (*ib.* p. 41) is impossible, the groups not forming a continuous sentence, but giving short phrases which can be arranged in a very variable order. An examination of the original may help to fix the reading.

12. See Mr. Petrie's ingenious explanation of the signs on p. 25.

13. The inscription is ⸻ ("northern corn"?) followed by a peculiar sign. Mr. Petrie supposes it to be the "measuring cord" ⸻ of the king, from the form of the staff on which it is engraved.

Pl. vii.A. 1. From a hunting scene. The jackal standard appears thus also in *R. T.*, i., Pl. xxxii. fig. 39.

2. Note ⸻, ⸻ ⸻, etc., as on *R. T.*, i., xv. 16 (see p. 41), xvii. 28.

3. Cf. *R. T.*, i., xi. 5 = xiv. 12:

4. Cf. *R. T.*, i., xi. 14 = xv. 16 left.

5. Cf. *R. T.*, i., xi. 6.

13. Note the emblems ⸻ passed through ⸻, much as in *Hierakonpolis*, Pl. ii.

Pl. viii. 2. Note the name of the king written ⸻ with the det. of the nose, as a variant of ⸻ in *R. T.*, i., xii. 2.

---

[1] Mr. Petrie informs me that the provenance of this fragment is not certain. The other fragment was apparently from the tomb of Semer-khet (U).

5. Cf. *R. T.*, i., xii. 1 = xvii. 26.

6. For another boat inscription of this king see *R. T.*, i., viii. 9. The (?) sign under Horus is compared by Mr. Petrie with that in Pl. xxvi. 59, xxvii. 102, and *R. T.*, i., x. 8, which he thinks may be a fishing-net.

7 joins the fragment *R. T.*, i., ix. 10.

8. The forked sign like ⚵ is not uncommon at this period in inscriptions of the earlier kings, *R. T.*, i., xiii. 2, xix. 9, 21, 22, 27, but disappears later. The occurrence of ⚵⚵ (sealings 27, 50) and ⚵⚵ (sealings 75, 78, etc.) suggests that the forked sign and ⚵ are only variants of each other, but it must be admitted that the differences are striking, and that there seems some distinction between the two in their employment: however, ⚵⚵⚵ is difficult to translate. The early engravers certainly show a tendency to incomplete outline, e.g. in ▯, ▯, xii. 3, ⌐, though possibly not without some warrant for it in the nature of the object. It seems very probable that 𓊵 Hetep-Sekhemuy is the correct reading.

12. Note the erased inscription mentioning the palace *s'-ḥ'* of the Horus Ra-neb with the subsequent inscription of king ⌐〜〜〜. See Mr. Petrie's interpretation, p. 26. The last sign is ⚵ *ys*.

13. Mr. Petrie suggests that the boat inscribed upon bowls (cf. viii. 6, *R. T.*, i., viii. 9) indicates that they belonged to the king's travelling outfit, just as others belonged to the palace, and others again to the tomb.

Pl. viii.A. 4 fits *R. T.*, i., viii. 3.

6. The standard shows the upper part of a bird.

7. = seal 164, Pl. xxi.

8. Apparently Upuat.

9. Neit, ⚵ and 𓈖.

Pl. x. 1 = ii. 4.

Pl. x. 2, xi. 2 = iii.A 5, 6. Here at the top we have, beside the Horus name of Menes, 𓀀, the ✚⚵⊗ symbol, a divine boat (of Sokaris?), a temple of Neit, etc. In the second row, behind

the bull and net (see Mr. Petrie's note), probably the ibis of Thoth on a shrine; compare *Hierakonpolis*, I., xxvi.B. The legend in the last line 𓆓𓏤𓅃 "who takes the throne of Horus," followed by 𓂝, with variations is found in *R. T.*, i., xv., etc.

Pl. xi. 1 = iii. 2.

Pl. xi. 2 = iii. 6, see x. 2.

Pl. xii. 1, 3, 4. The colours, red and black, used in the hieroglyphs on these tablets, are not altogether arbitrary. The ⬭, ⊔ and ▽ are appropriately red, as later. With the first group on 1 ("washing of the king's hand," Petrie) compare v. 13, 14, viii. 12, also the note on ii. 8. 3 contains the common group ⌐⌐ (unless it be ⌐⌐ *mz*), cf. v.A 16, also ⚵(?) ⊔. 3 contains the name of the palace (?) ⚵⬭ Qed-hotep of Zer, occurring also in an inscription of Merpaba, *R. T.*, i., vi. 8. ⌐⌐ (hardly ⌐⌐ *mz*) is found in v.A 16, and on the sealings 20 (?), 40, 41, 118, while the whole group ⌐⌐⚵(?) ⊔ closely resembles those on the sealings 5—7 and 129.

5. The sign beneath Anubis in the third instance appears to be ⚵ *ys*.

6. = viii. 3.

SEALINGS.

48. Pl. xiii. No. 89 = ii. 1. The other instances of the Horus name ⌐⌐ figured in the plate are from jars.

91, 92. Note the separation of Nar (?) from Mer on the sealings; the signs are awkward to arrange together in a rectangular compartment, see the artistic grouping on the slate *Hierakonpolis*, I., Pl. xxix., and above ii. 3, *R. T.*, i., iv. 2.

93. Here ⌐⌐ alternates with the *Ka*-name Nar-mer, suggesting that the latter may be Menes, in the same way that No. 2, 109, may give the names of Zet and Zer; but such evidence is very far from trustworthy, otherwise it would prove that Aha was also named

both (No. 99) and (De Morgan, fig. 558), whereas the tablet of Naqada clearly gives his name with royal title, viz. (Menes), or at least some very similar sign. Instances of the personal name with the Horus name of a king on one seal are those of Den (pl. vii. 5, 6), and of Azab (*R. T.*, i., seal 57); and the indirect cases of Azab (seals 58, 59), and Semerkhet (seal 72). The absence of the title before the names of Ta and Ath (in contrast to Az-ab, No. 57) is not in itself significant, as that title never appears before the reign of Den.

Pl. xiv. 98, 99 were found also in the Naqada tomb (De Morgan, *Recherches*, ii., figs. 556, 557). For the group cf. No. 116 and *ḥ ·t* "tomb" (?) in No. 53 (*R. T.*, i.).

Pl. xv. 111. cf. the sealings of Mer-neit, *R. T.*, i., xx., and the stelae of the time of Den and later. (?) may be "keeper of the rams (or goats)."

112. "Keeper of the pools"?

113. Compare Pl. ii. 15. We have here the group of the three plovers (*Ptahhetep*, I., 20) alternating with which may also be followed by or by . The plovers occur very frequently on objects from the Naqada tomb (De Morgan, *Rech.*, ii., figs. 517, 525, 598—601, 661, 662, 667, 673. Mr. Thompson considers it a proper name. Note the remarkable symbolism of the bird in *Hierakonpolis*, I., xxvi. c. 1, and its occurrence on stelae *R. T.*, i., xxxi. 1 (?), 3.

Pl. xvi. 115, 116. Note the lion or leopard with bent bars on his back as on the tablets of Hesy, also *sḥ* and a shrine, which in 116 seems shaped to recall . In 116 also the signs East and North are in juxtaposition (making North-east ?), as in No. 37.

121—24. Cf. 10—15 and 18—20; in 124 we seem to have in the enclosure, in 20 takes the place of , but cf. 136.

Pl. xvii. 128. Cf. *R. T.*, i., 8, 9.

129. For the group of four bars cf. 122, 143, etc., and better 142.

134. Cf. 17, 24, 25. is probably a private name. Beyond is Anubis *ḫnt-sḥ-ntr*.

Pl. xviii. 136. For the town name cf. 45—47, 49, 50, 149, 153, 159, 161—63.

139. The city-name occurs on Nos. 23, 52, 53, 55, 56, 139, 150, 154, 155, 156 (?).

141. occurs on Nos. 47, 48, 54, 63—65, 83, 84, 118 (?), 141, 149, 163, 179, 199, De Morgan, *Rech.*, ii., fig. 784. There is every degree between the short of No. 48 and the tall straight of No. 199. The variations are made to suit the requirements of the space to be filled, for the decorative quality of the seal was clearly a matter of the first importance—compare Hemaka on Nos. 53, 56. Mr. Thompson would read it as *ḥtp* in every case. The sign which occurs on 201 has a narrower base; in 47, 54, 163, and De Morgan 784 the "offerings" are defined as : in 47, 48, 141, 149, 163 the group is increased by of the governors, once (149) by . In every instance the title is associated with a city-name, sometimes alone (Nos. 47, 83, 179, 199) and sometimes with (Nos. 54, 64, 84, 149, 163). In 178 takes a place corresponding to that of in 179.

Pl. xix. 146. occurs in Nos. 6, 18—21, 46, 67, 69, 81, 131—32, 146—48, 150, sometimes accompanied only by the royal name, in others in association with other titles, most commonly with . As it is found under five kings of the Ist Dynasty, it clearly denoted an office of some permanence. The swimming sign is found in the Pyramids (N. 652) exactly as in these, including the arch of drops over the swimmer. From *Siut*, tomb v., l. 22, we gather that the royal children were regularly taught to swim *nb·t*; the sign is also used to express *nb·t*, to smelt or melt metals.

149. " occurs on 27, 44, 45, 50, 55, 66,

70, 75, 78, 138 (?), 140, 149, 153, 158, 161, 173; and, except in the last three cases, always is in immediate connection with the Horus name of a king, six of whom are thus named. It must therefore be a title, and probably one implying royal favour rather than an office of administration; perhaps 'ruling in the king's heart' is meant, cf. later 〔〕 ~~~ ⌐, etc." H. T.

" ⌐ *ᶜd-mᵣ*, according to Brugsch, 'inspector of canals'; according to Maspero, a high fiscal official. A frequent title in the Old Kingdom, and in these early sealings at least always in connection with the name of a city. It occurs fifteen times, viz. on 24, 49, 56, 64—67, 84, 149, 153, 154, 158, 161, 163, 178." H. T.

153. "The group 〔〕 is probably a proper name, as will be seen by comparing this sealing with No. 161, where we have the name of the chancellor Hemaka (see *R. T.*, i., p. 41) occupying a corresponding position. The name occurs also on No. 29 (*R. T.*, i., Pl. xxi., reign of Merneit), and No. 149 (◎ omitted): nos. 149 and 153 belonging to the reign of Den." H. T.

Pl. xx. 158. From a comparison with No. 161 it seems evident that 〔〕 is a proper name, Mezr-k'. For the reading, see SETHE, *Ä. Z.*, xxx. 52." H. T.

49. Pl. xxi. 164. Mr. Petrie quotes a seal in his own collection with the Horus name 〔〕 (*Hist.*, i., 2nd ed., p. 24). This he believes to combine the two royal names 〔〕 and 〔〕. It will be observed that on the Abydos seals and elsewhere (except the later cartouches in the tomb of Shera) the former is invariably a Horus name (for Lower Egypt?), the latter a Set name (for Upper Egypt?). On Mr. Petrie's seal we may at any rate recognise the Horus name Sekhem-ab. In the next series (Kha-Sekhemui) the deities are associated over the single Horus-Set name, which name also itself signifies the union in a remarkable manner. Here, with the Horus name, we have a southern seal 〔〕, probably to be read *ḫtm ᶜ nb Qmᶜ*, "seal of every document (?) of the South country" (or for "seal" read "chancellor"); but Set wears the crown of Upper Egypt in 179.

165. "〔〕 *tp ḥr stn*, 'next after the king' (ERMAN, *Aegypten*, p. 82, otherwise MASPERO, *Études Ég.*, ii., 266), very common in the Old Kingdom." H. T.

〔〕 *ys zfᵓw*, "office of the fatlings (?)." According to our present evidence this appellation or title commences in the IInd Dynasty. Where the sealing is complete it is usually in connection with 〔〕 (201), 〔〕 (167, 174, 183), or 〔〕 (192). Once we have 〔〕 (166). The same combination as here recurs in 195.

176. The first group here should be the title of priest of the goddess figured below, i.e., possibly Isis, according to the second group 〔〕, though her headdress seems to be that of a Nile-goddess. Her name 〔〕, in fact, seems to occur again at her feet.

In 178, 179, 199, 200 (DE MORGAN, *Rech.*, ii., figs. 816, 819), we have a group 〔〕, the bird in which is very variable, attached to male deities, in 179 Set, in 178 Osiris (?), in 199 Shu (?).

Pl. xxii. 178—80. The name of the place seems to be 〔〕 "the ships of the king."

184. "Chancellor of Northern tribute (?)."

190. A fragmentary specimen was published last year as 87.

〔〕, in 201 〔〕, in DE MORGAN, *Rech.*, ii., fig. 820, 〔〕. 〔〕 is a word for sealing. "Sealing (?) of everything": in 201 〔〕 must mean "in good condition." Mr. Thompson would make 〔〕 = *szᵓwty*, "sealer" (= 〔〕 *Ä. Z.*, 1894, p. 65, 1898, p. 145, 1899, p. 86), and perhaps the title of an official is more appropriate than the name of an office or act of administration or of the seal itself.

Pl. xxiii. 191. The name of the king has been interpreted very appropriately by Maspero. In detail one might suggest that ⚬⚬ *Sekhemui* (?) may be intended for *Shm·ty*, the name of the Pshenty or double crown ⚭ : we should then read " the double crown Pshenty, in which the deities unite (or are satisfied)."

Vine trellis ⚭ occurs in seven sealings, viz. Nos. 68, 191—93, 196, 202, 204. In five of these cases with the sign ⊔ before it for ⊔ ⊘, found before groups of vines or trees, L. *D.*, ii. 61, Duem., *Res.*, ii. (Tomb of Ty), " garden," " orchard," later written ⊔ ⚭ ⚭ ⚭. In some instances it is combined with a further group, variously written ⚭ (?) ⚭ 68, ⚭ ⚭. 191, *k'nw stn pr dšr*, *k'nw pr dšr pr stn* " royal orchards of the king's house, red house." In 192 and 196 we have the " orchard of the ⚭ ⚬ or ⚭ ⊛, *khent*-garden of the king, red house." In Maspero, *Ét. Ég.*, ii. 269, there is the title ⚭ ⚭ ⚭ ⚭. In 29, 33, we may have mention of the royal cellars; in 73, 74, 77, of the beer or wine jars.

⚭ occurs in Nos. 68, 191, 192, 196, 204 (?), 206, almost exclusively in the IInd Dynasty. Mr. Thompson suggests that the " white house " and the " red house " refer to the administration of the South and the North respectively, comparing the colours of the ⚭ and the ⚭.

192. Mr. Thompson renders this " superintendent (?) of live-stock tribute of the Red House, and of the gardens and vineyards of the king of the North and South." Note the rare form of the royal title ⚭ ⚭, which occurs also in 196, and on the Palermo stone B. 1. 3.

193 = De Morgan, 818. The nome of Memphis seems here to be named.

197 = De Morgan, 817.

⚭ ⚭ " superintendent of embankment (?),"

(*Ptahhetep*, I., p. 26), a common title in the Old Kingdom and continued later.

198. " ⚭ *pr ḥr nd* and ⚭ ⚭ *ḥrp 'd 'ḥ* are two titles analogous to titles also closely associated in the early tomb of *Pḥ-nfr* described by Maspero (*Ét. Ég.*, ii., 259, 260). There they appear as ⚭ ⚭ ' superintendent of the mill (?),' and ⚭ ⚭ ⚭ which Maspero translates, ' directeur de la maison des graisses de bœuf.' " H. T. Note also ⚭ in the same seal.

199. Cf. De Morgan, 819.

200. Cf. De Morgan, 816.

201. Cf. De Morgan, 820, and No. 190 above.

Pl. xxiv. 207. ⚭ is probably a proper name. The group ⚭ ⚭ ⚭ " plough " (note the full spelling) occurs also on Nos. 208, 213, 217A (?), and further on a cylinder (F. P. Coll.).

210. Cf. De Morgan, fig. 821, Borchardt, Naville, and Sethe (*Ä. Z.*, xxxvi. 142). " Mother of the king's children (*mwt msw-stn*), Hepenmaat; if she say anything, it is done for her, Hepenmaat; chancellor (?) of the carpentry (or ship-building, *wḥrt*), Hepenmaat."

Pl. xxvii., xxviii. *Stelae.* Many of the names on these are easily legible. They are mostly of women. The cross × probably stands for the crossed arrows of Neith, cf. Nos. 9, 11 in *R. T.*, i., xxxi. In 96 and 129 there would seem to be the title ⚭ ⚭ *w'rt·w*, so common in the Middle Kingdom, but the personages are women. The most remarkable phrase or title occurs on the series 120—125, with 21 in the former volume; viz. ⚭ ⚭ (?) ⚭ ⚭ ⚭, followed in each case by the person's name. I do not see any clue to the meaning beyond the name of Den contained in it. Here are very clear examples of the use of determinatives in ⚭ and ⚭ for man and woman respectively. Possibly these are the earliest determinative signs used in the hieroglyphic system.

INDEX.

PRINTED BY GILBERT AND RIVINGTON, LIMITED, ST. JOHN'S HOUSE, CLERKENWELL, E.C.

1. SEAL OF KA.
Tomb B. 7.

2. UNKNOWN.   3, 6. NARMER, ALABASTER.   4. EBONY.   5. IVORY.
Tomb B. 17.   Tomb B. 13.   Tomb B. 18.

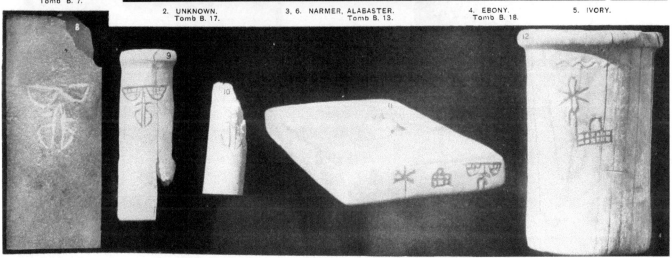

8. SAM, BASALT.   9, 10. IVORY.   11, 12. IVORY LID AND VASE, SAM, NEIT-HOTEP. TOMB O.2.

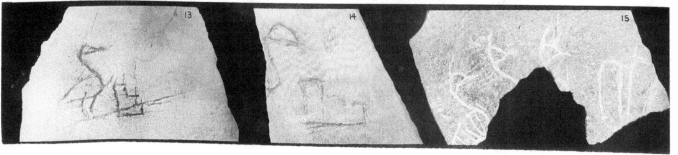

13. POTTERY.   14. ALABASTER. B. 10.   15. SERPENTINE. B. 10.

B9 ; 1.   B10 ; 3.   B14 ; 8, 9, 10, 11, 12, 13.   B15 ; 7.   B18 ; 6.   B18 and 19 ; 5.

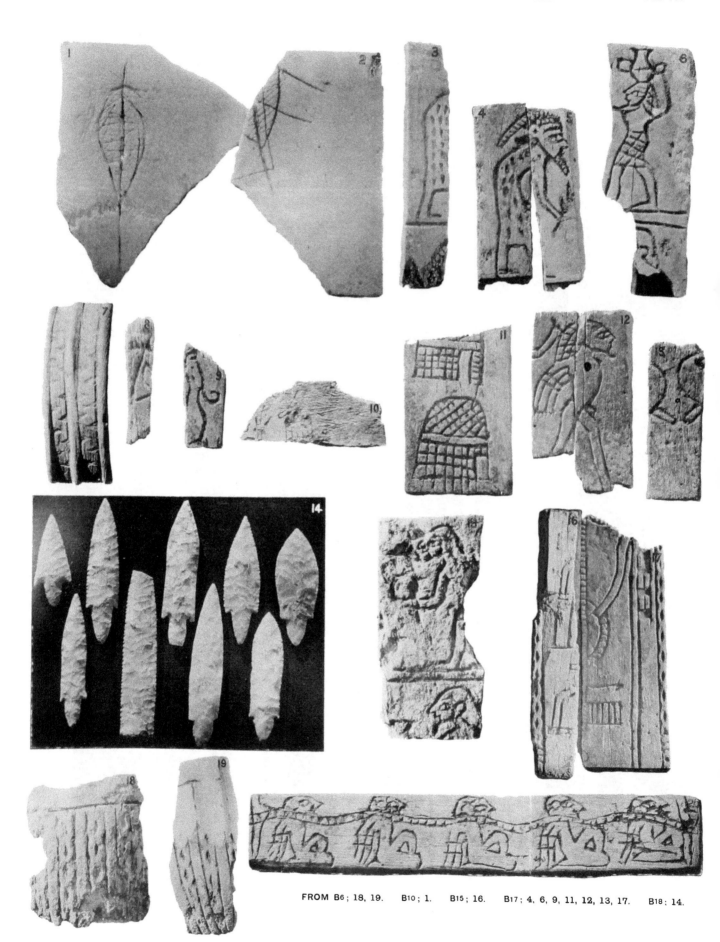

FROM B6; 18, 19.   B10; 1.   B15; 16.   B17; 4, 6, 9, 11, 12, 13, 17.   B18; 14.

1—3. IVORY LABELS. 4. IVORY BOX. 5. STONE VASE. 6. IVORY WAND.

7. IVORY CUP 9—10. WOODEN LABELS. 11. EBONY SEAL.

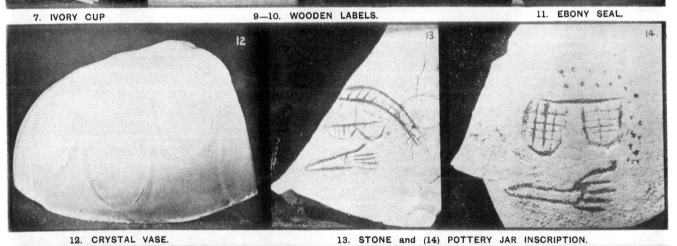

12. CRYSTAL VASE. 13. STONE and (14) POTTERY JAR INSCRIPTION.

15. CARVED MARBLE. 16. CHARCOAL. 17. CLAY SEALING. 18. ON STONE BOWL.

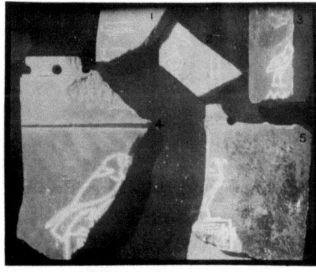

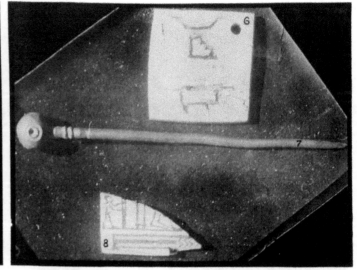

1, 2. STONE.   3—5. IVORY.   7. PIN OF GOLD ALLOY.   6, 8. IVORY.

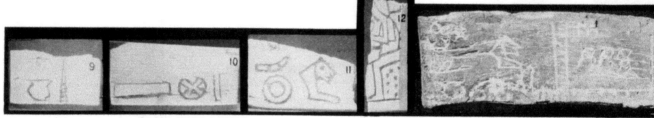

9—12. IVORY LABELS.   13. WOOD TABLET.

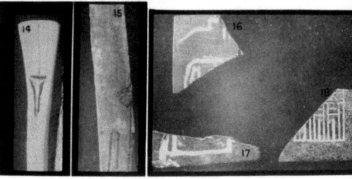

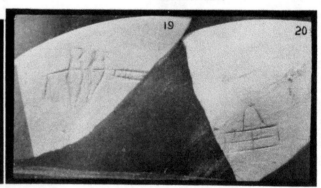

14—18. IVORY PIECES.   19, 20. STONE BOWL PIECES.

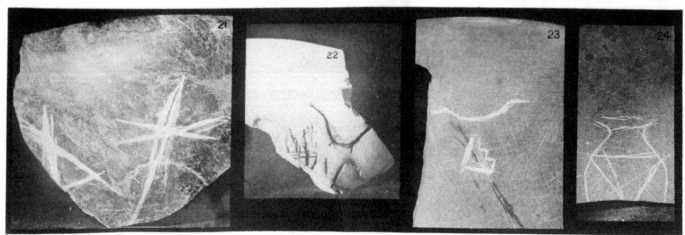

ON STONE BOWLS.

1. PIECE OF BRACELET. 2. SERPENT HEAD.   3, 4. IVORY LIONS, GAMING PIECES (1 : 1).

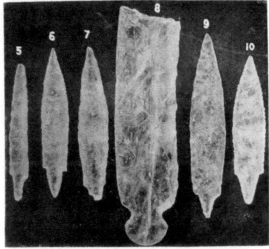

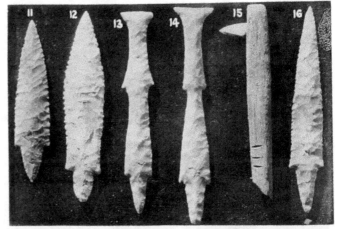

11—14, 16. FLINT ARROWS.   15. FLINT IN WOOD.

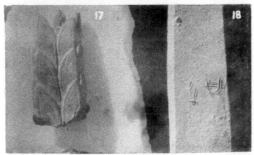

5—10. CRYSTAL ARROWS AND KNIFE.

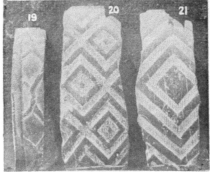

IVORY CORN.   COPPER CHISEL.   19—21. IVORY BRACELETS.   ON IVORY VASE.

23—26. COPPER TOOLS. GRAVE O.31 (1 : 2).   27. MARBLE VASE.

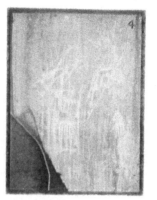

IVORY.   CHARCOAL.   EBONY.

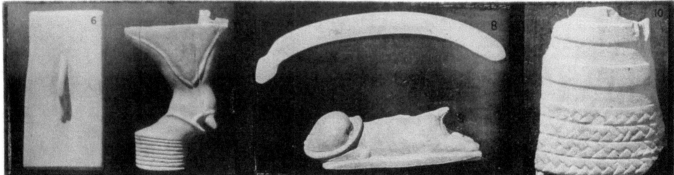

1 : 2.   IVORIES.   4 : 3.

1 : 4.   11—13. IVORY.   15, 16. **WOOD.**   4 : 3. AGATE   CLAY SEALING.   19. GOLD.   21. ELECTRUM.

22—24. MARBLE.   25, 26. BROWN SCHIST.

1, 3—6. IVORY LABELS.

2. WOODEN LABEL.

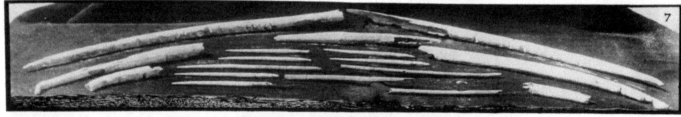

1 : 5. HORN BOWS AND REED ARROWS WITH IVORY TIPS.

8—13. CARVINGS ON WOOD, NOW CHARCOAL; WITH REVERSES.

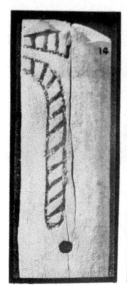

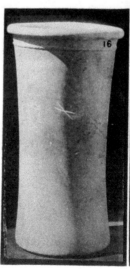

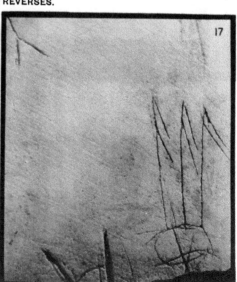

IVORY INLAY.

IVORY BULL'S LEG. T. 5.

2 : 5. SLATE VASE. T. 5.

ON ALABASTER. (? SITE.)

1—3. IVORY LABELS OF KING QA—SEN.

4, 5, IVORY LABELS, and 6, 7, STONE BOWLS OF KING QA—SEN.

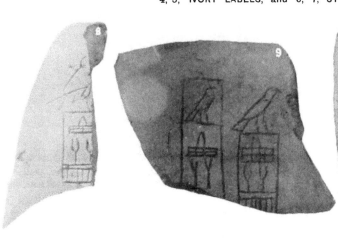
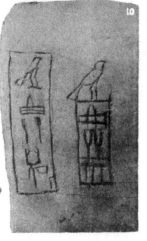
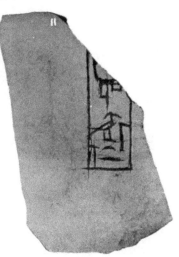

8—11. STONE BOWLS OF KING HOTEP-AHAUI (TOMB OF PERABSEN).

12. BOWL OF KING RANEB, RE-INSCRIBED BY (13) KING NETEREN (TOMB OF PERABSEN).

1—3. STONE BOWLS OF MERPABA.

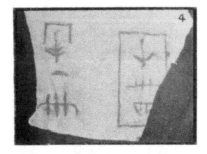

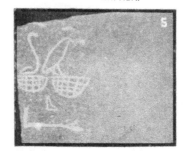

4—6. STONE BOWLS OF QA—SEN.

7. SEALING OF PERABSEN.   8, 9. STONE BOWLS, SITE UNCERTAIN.

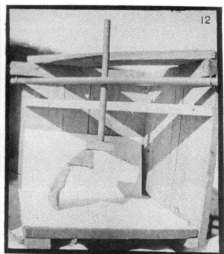

10—12. VASE FRAGMENTS SUPERPOSED IN FRAME FOR DRAWING RESTORATIONS.

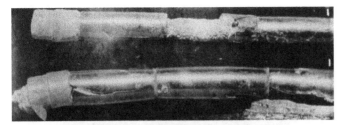

PORTIONS OF SARD AND GOLD SCEPTRE.

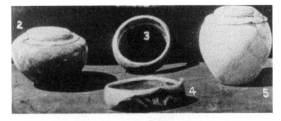

(2 : 5) GOLD-CAPPED VASES. GOLD BRACELETS.

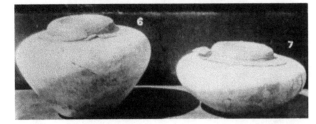

2 : 5. GOLD-CAPPED VASES OF WHITE MARBLE.

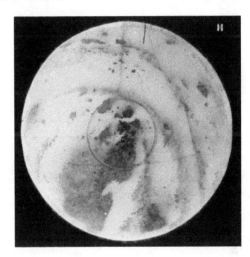

1 : 3. DIORITE BOWL.

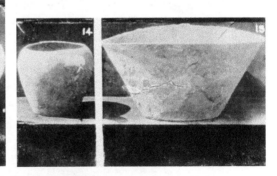

MARBLE BASKET-WORK BOWL.

(1 : 5) COPPER BOWLS AND EWERS.

PIECE OF MENDED BOWL WITH GOLD PINS.

CARVED IVORY.

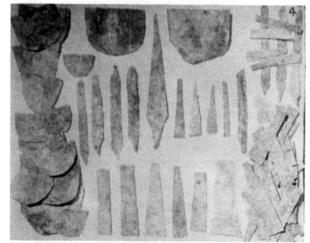

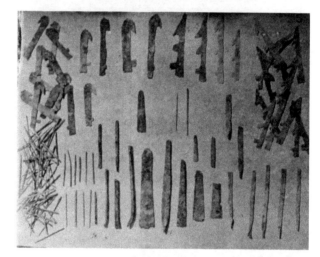

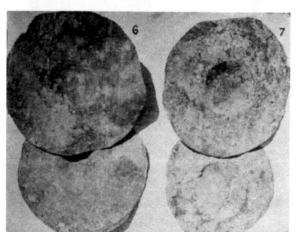

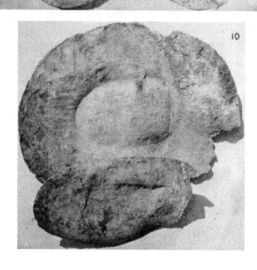

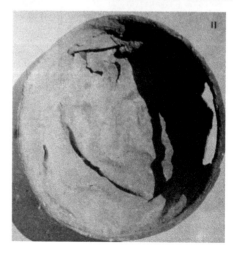

A·Z· xxxiv· 160

3

On back of Nº 2,
red paint.

1

B 18

2

red & black paint
On back of No. 2

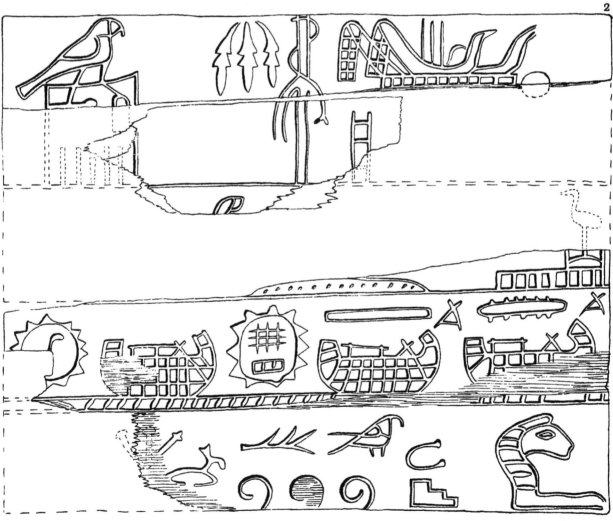

O.

PIECE OF WOODEN FIGURE.
PAINTED ON BREAST
WITH NECKLACES.
C.

O

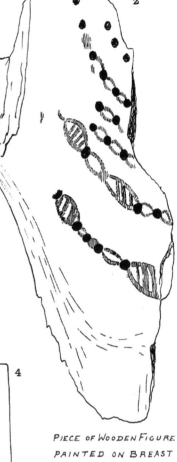

B18

4:3

WOODEN CYLINDER INSCRIBED IN INK.   Q

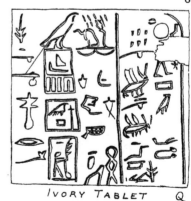

IVORY TABLET   Q

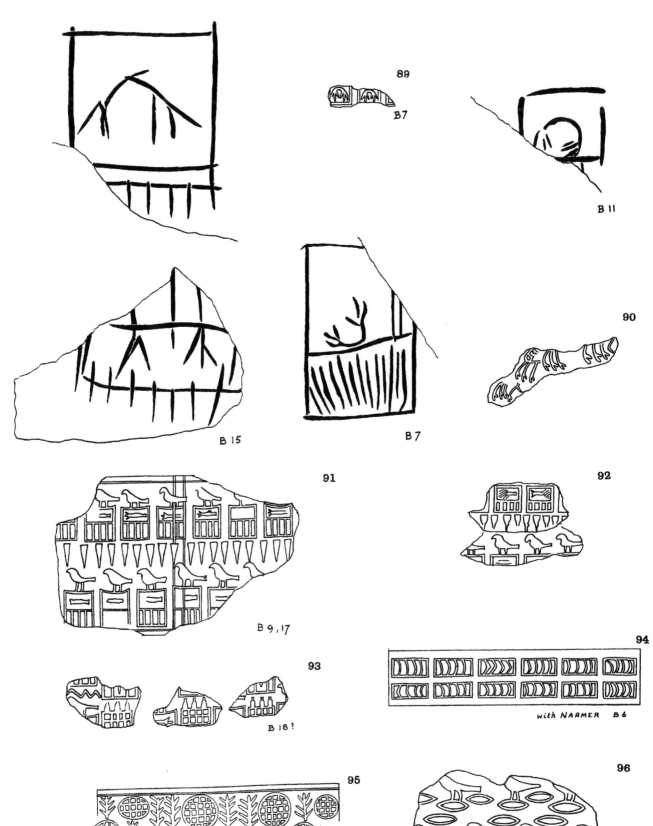

89

B 7

B 11

B 15

B 7

90

91

B 9, 17

92

93

B 18?

94

with NARMER   B 6

95

B 16

96

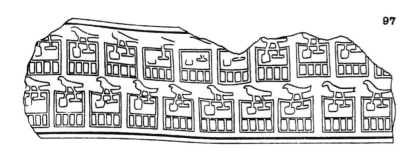

97

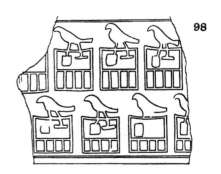

98

99

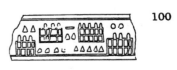

100

101

102

103

104

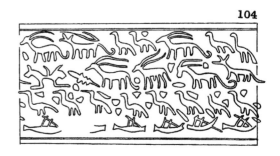

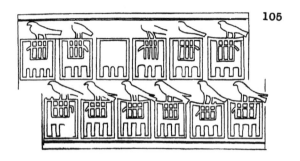

105

4:3

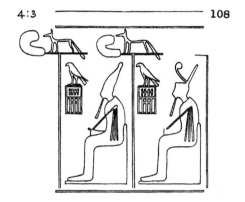

108

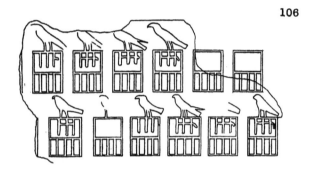

106

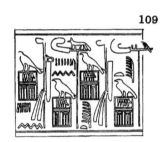

109

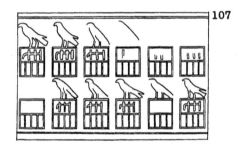

107

110

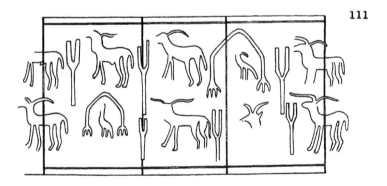

111

112

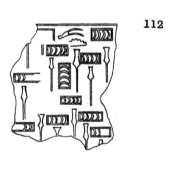

113

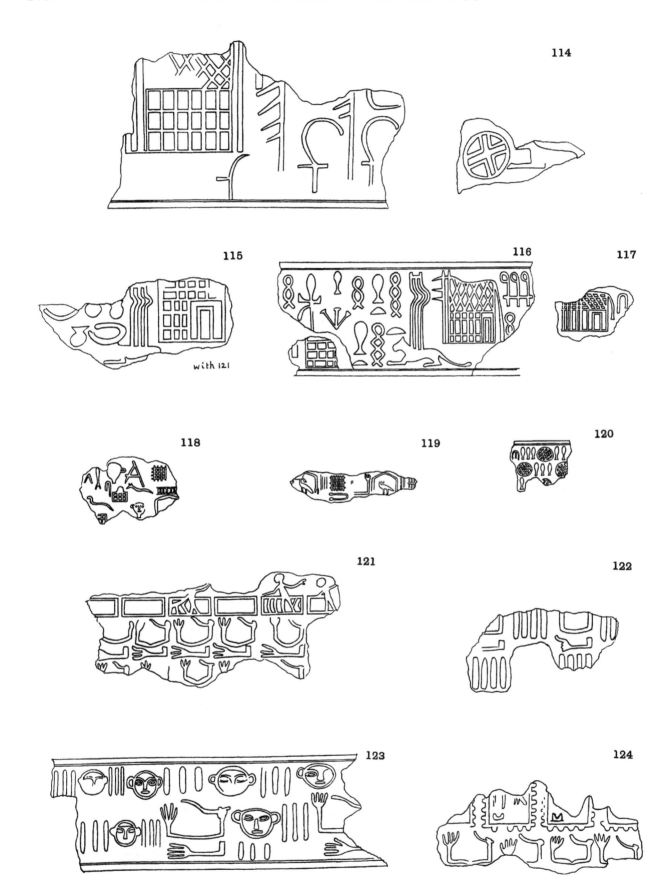

114

115

with 121

116

117

118

119

120

121

122

123

124

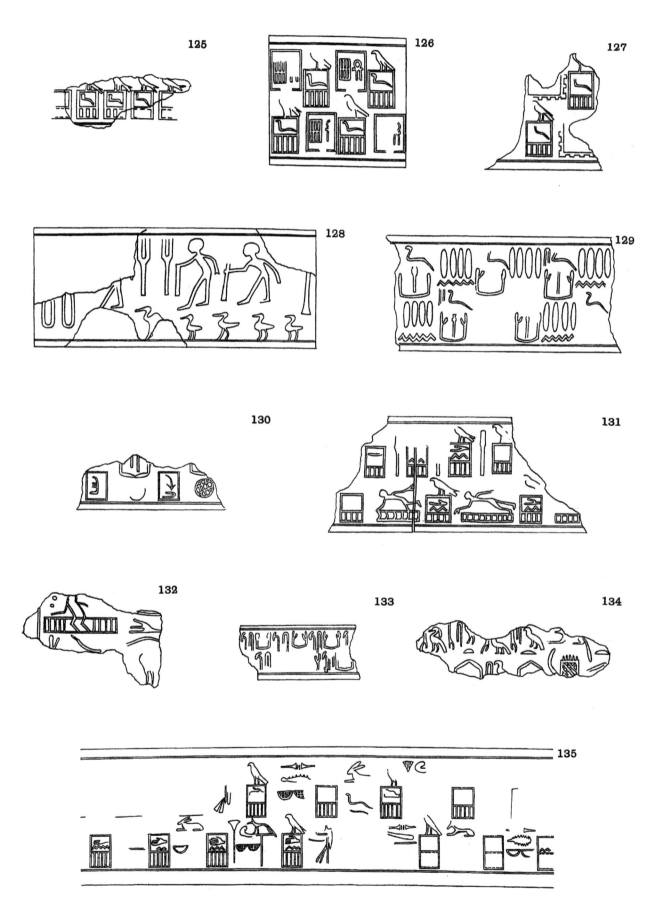

136

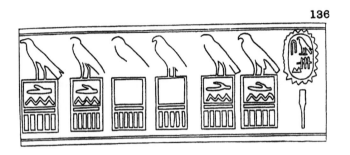

137

138

139

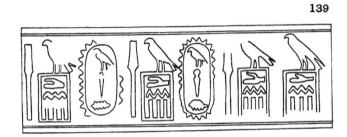

140

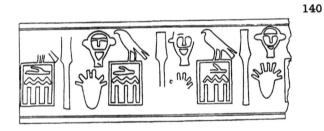

141

142

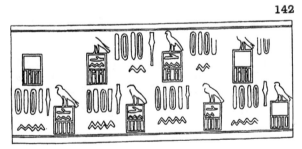

143

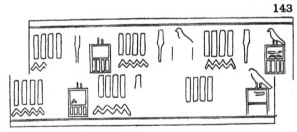

144

145

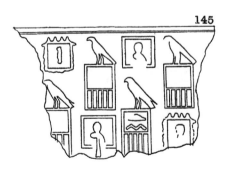

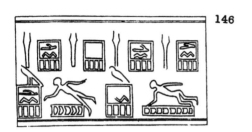

146

147

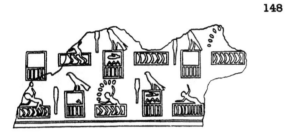

148

149

150

151

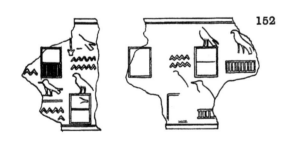

152

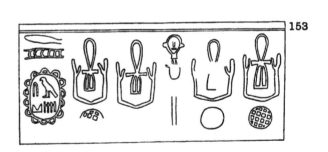

153

154

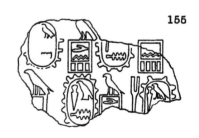

155

156

157

158

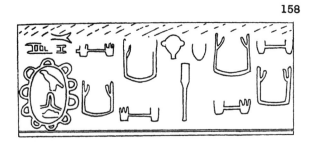

159

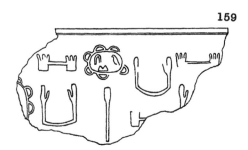

4:3   160

161

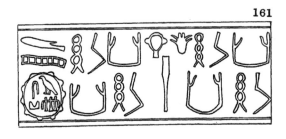

162

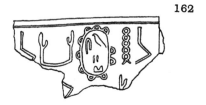

163

No 54 completed.

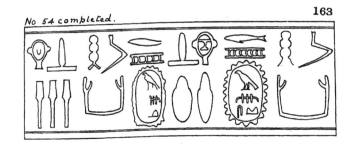

164

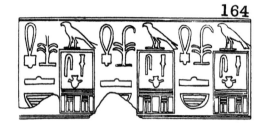

165

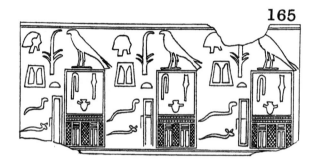

166

167

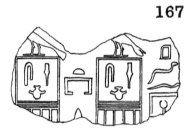

168

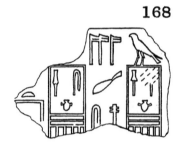

169

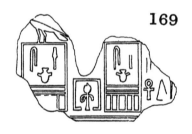

170

171

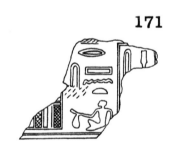

172

173

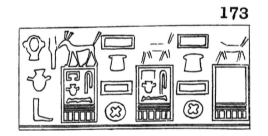

174

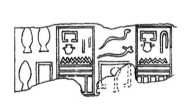

175

176

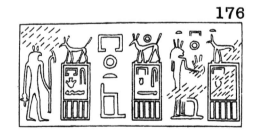

177

178

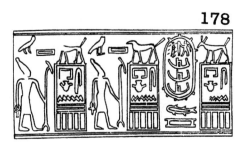

No. 88 completed   **179**

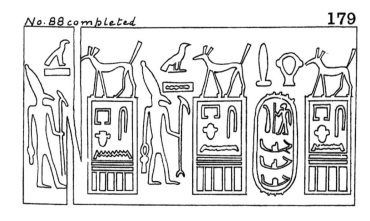

180

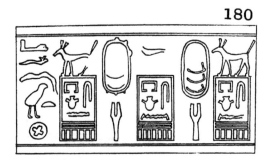

181

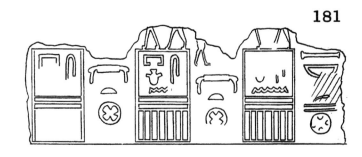

182

183

184

185

186

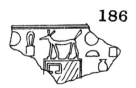

187

188

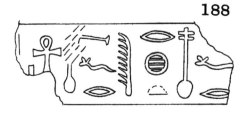

189

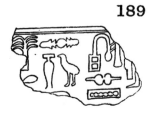

190

191

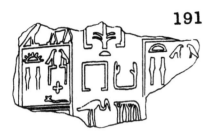

192

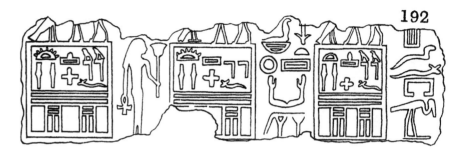

193

194

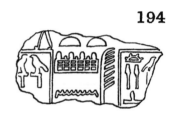

195

196

197

N. end

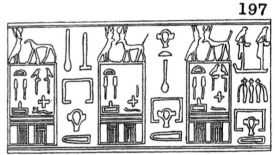

198

199

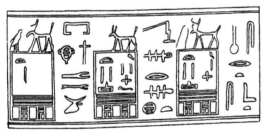

200

201

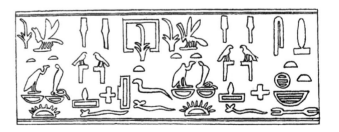

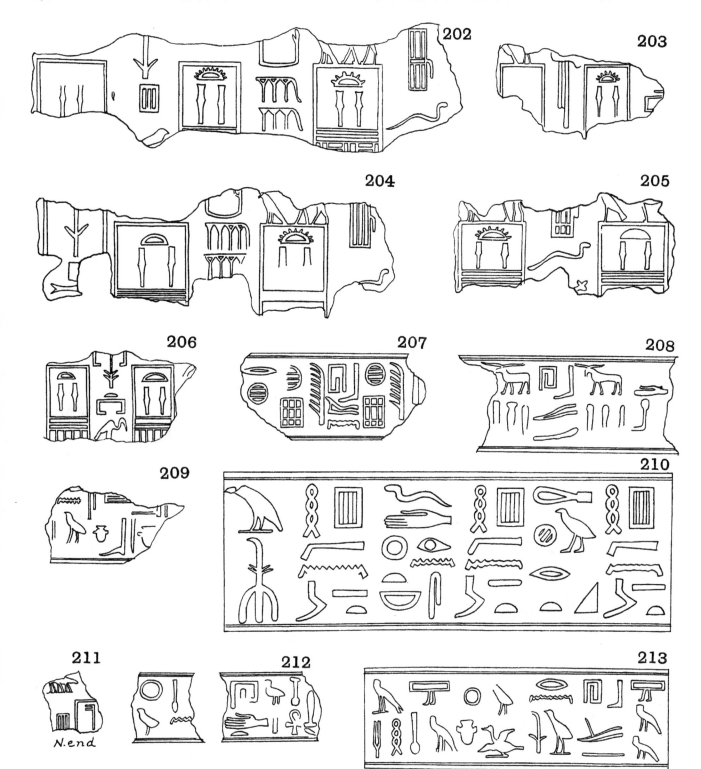

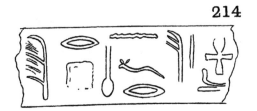

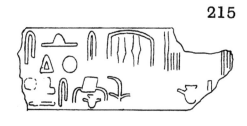

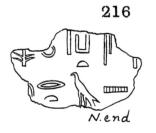

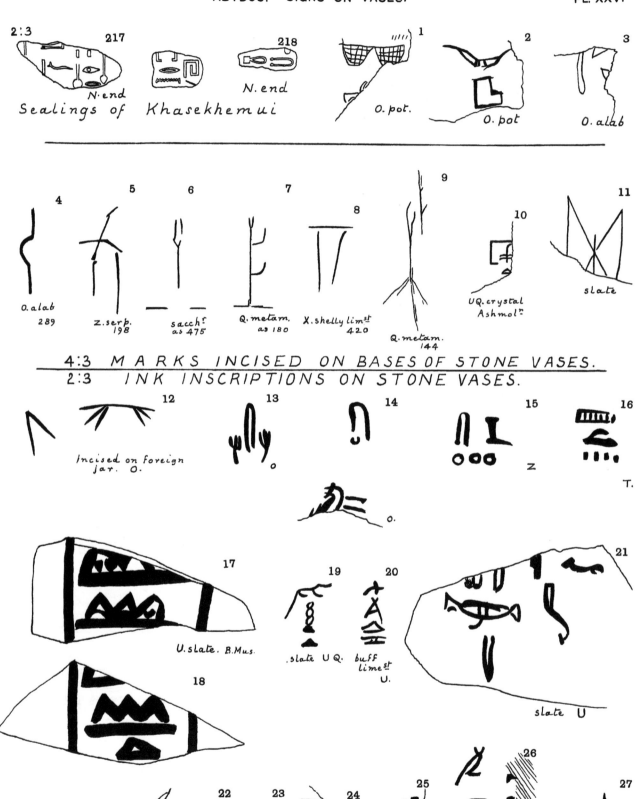

2:3

217

N. end

218

N. end

Sealings of Khasekhemui

1

O. pot.

2

O. pot

3

O. alab

4

O. alab
289

5

6

7

8

9

10

UQ. crystal
Ashmolⁿ

11

slate

z. serp.
198

sacch⁻
as 475

Q. metam.
as 180

X. shelly lim⁻st
420

Q. metam.
144

4:3 MARKS INCISED ON BASES OF STONE VASES.
2:3 INK INSCRIPTIONS ON STONE VASES.

12

Incised on foreign
jar. O.

13

O.

14

15

z

16

T.

O.

17

U. slate. B. Mus.

18

19

.slate UQ.

20

buff
lim⁻st
U.

21

slate U

22

outside
on bowl of thin slate

inside
Q.

23

Q

24

Q.

25

Q.

26

alab.

Q

27

alab.

STELES FROM AROUND THE TOMB OF DEN-SETUI, PLS. XXX. XXXA.

Same unsanded.

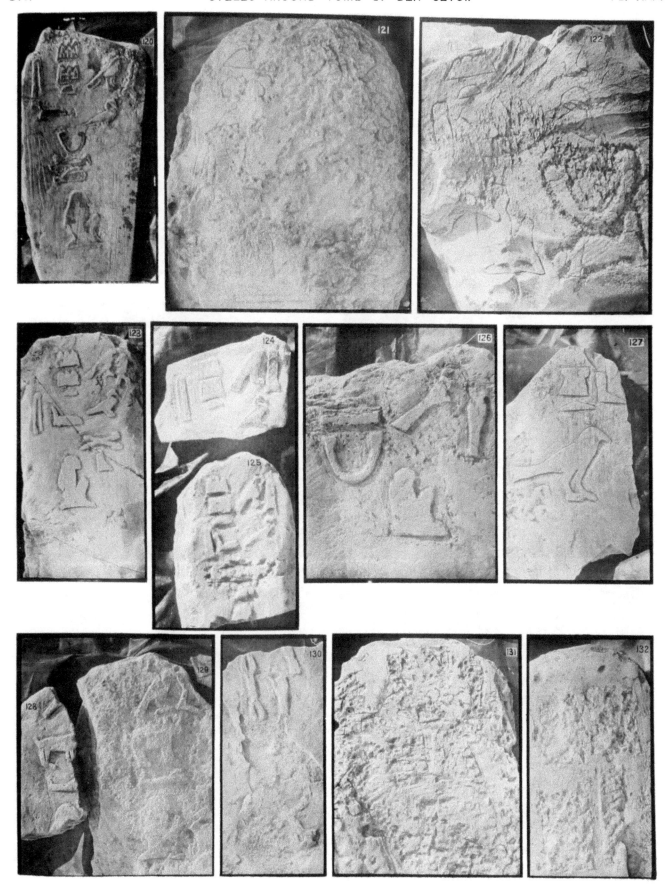

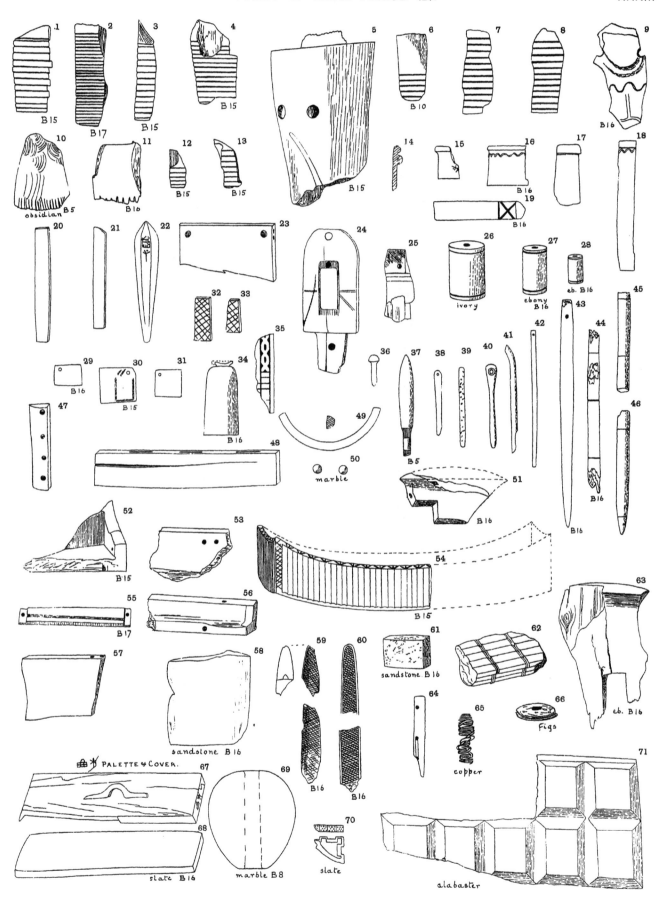

PALETTE & COVER.

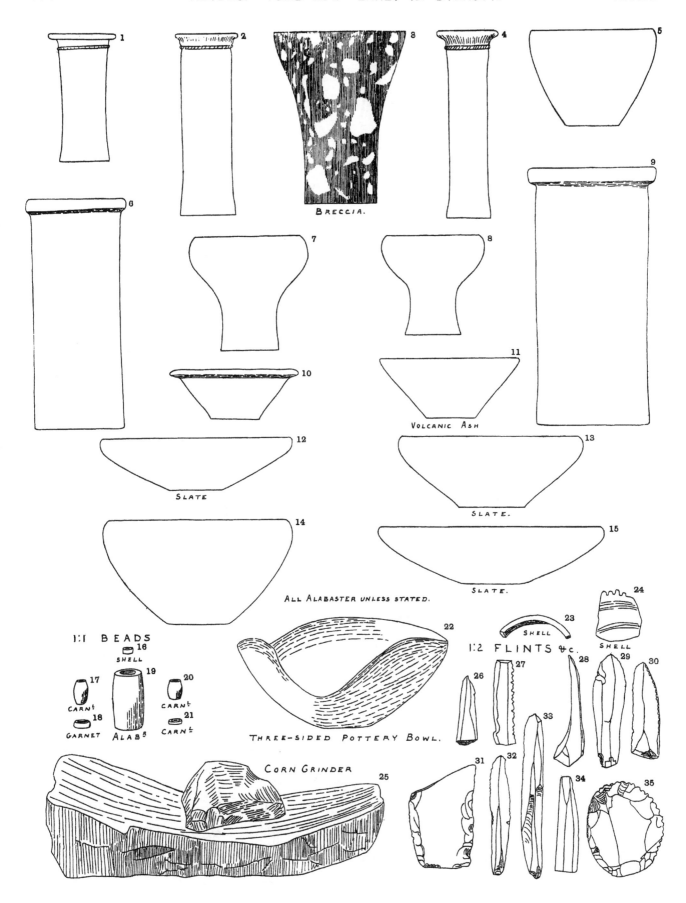

BRECCIA.

VOLCANIC ASH

SLATE

SLATE.

SLATE.

ALL ALABASTER UNLESS STATED.

1:1 BEADS

16 SHELL

17 CARN^t

19 ALAB^s

20 CARN^t

18 GARNET

21 CARN^t

THREE-SIDED POTTERY BOWL.

22

23 SHELL

24 SHELL

1:2 FLINTS &c.

CORN GRINDER

25

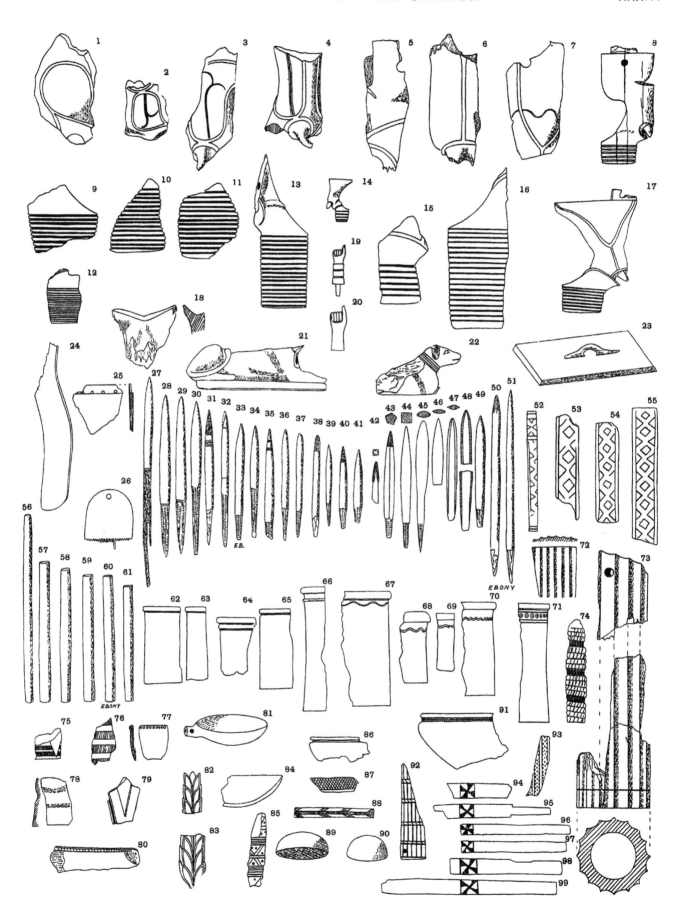

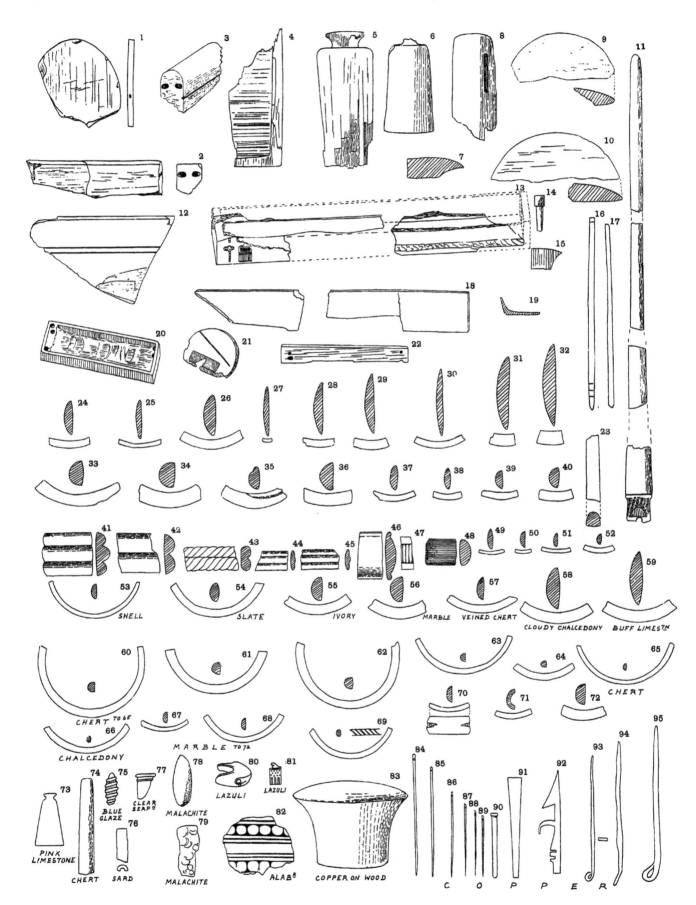

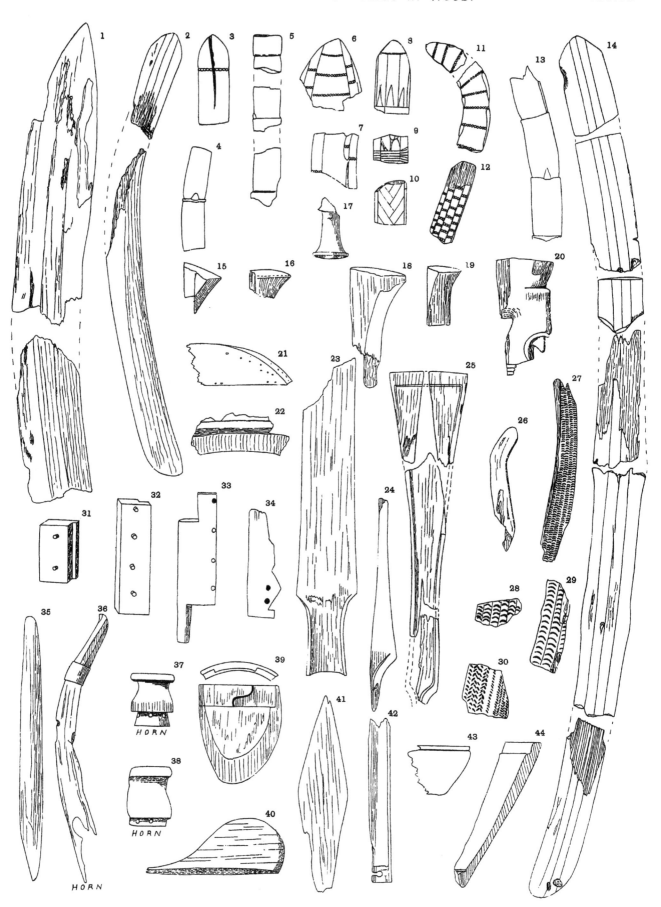

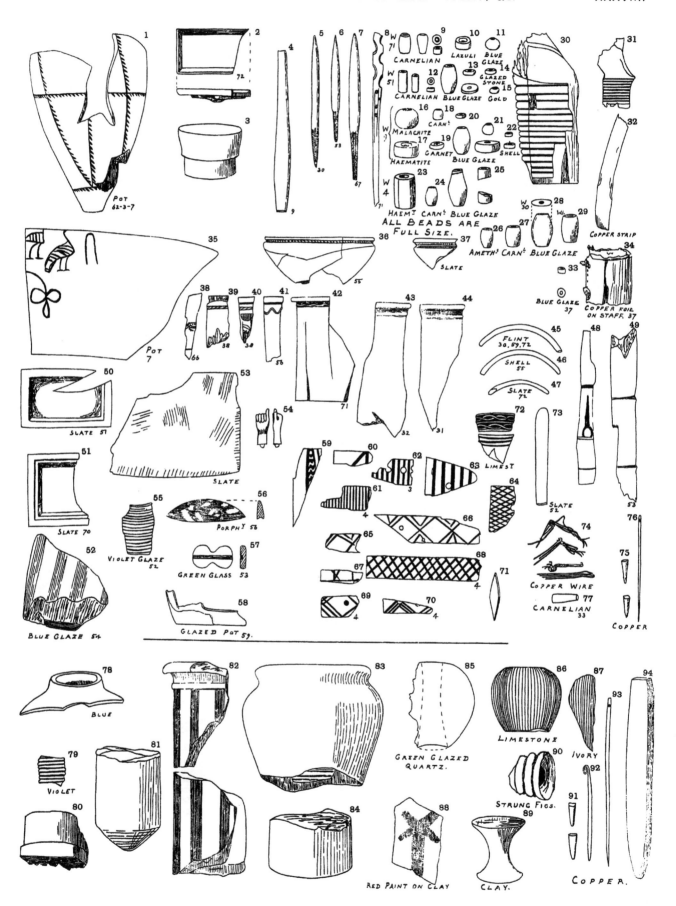

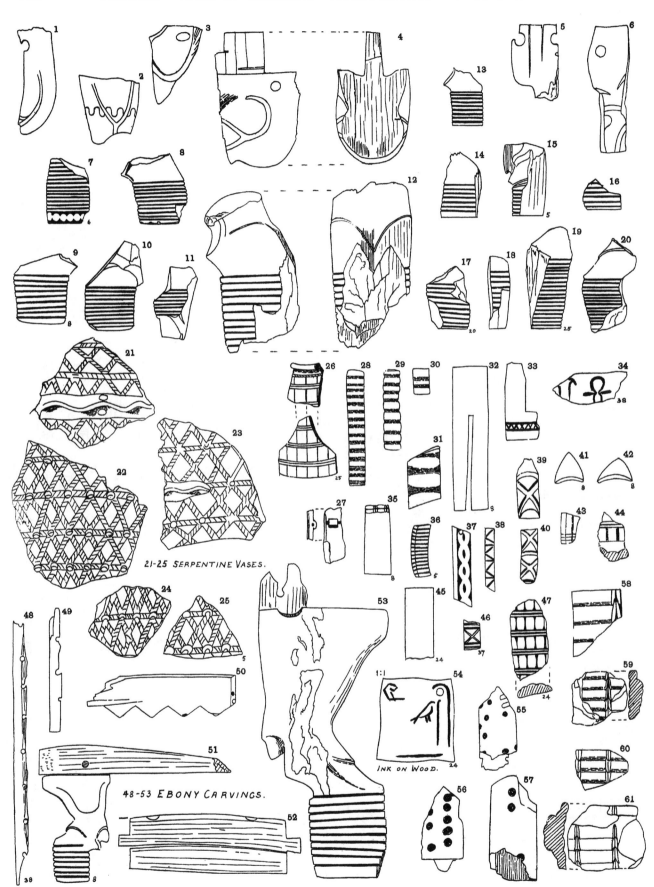

21-25 SERPENTINE VASES.

48-53 EBONY CARVINGS.

INK ON WOOD.

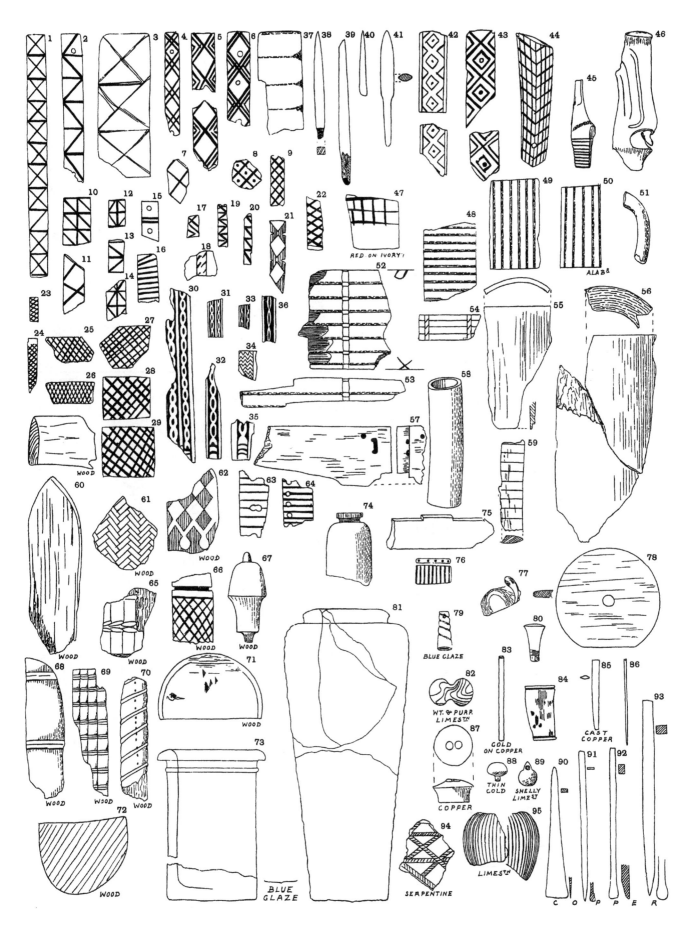

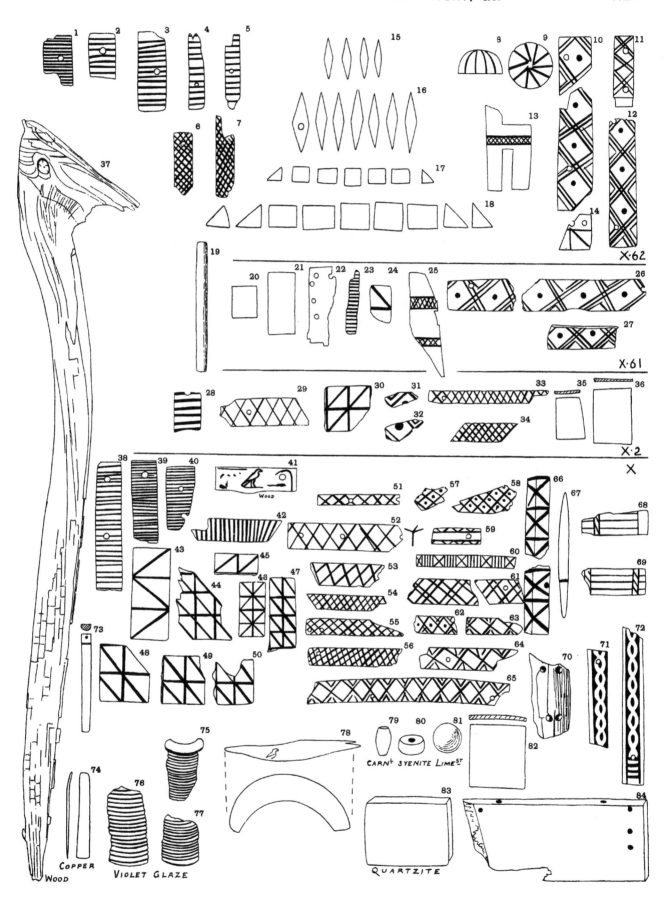

CARN.ᵗ SYENITE LIME.ˢᵀ

COPPER
WOOD

VIOLET GLAZE

QUARTZITE

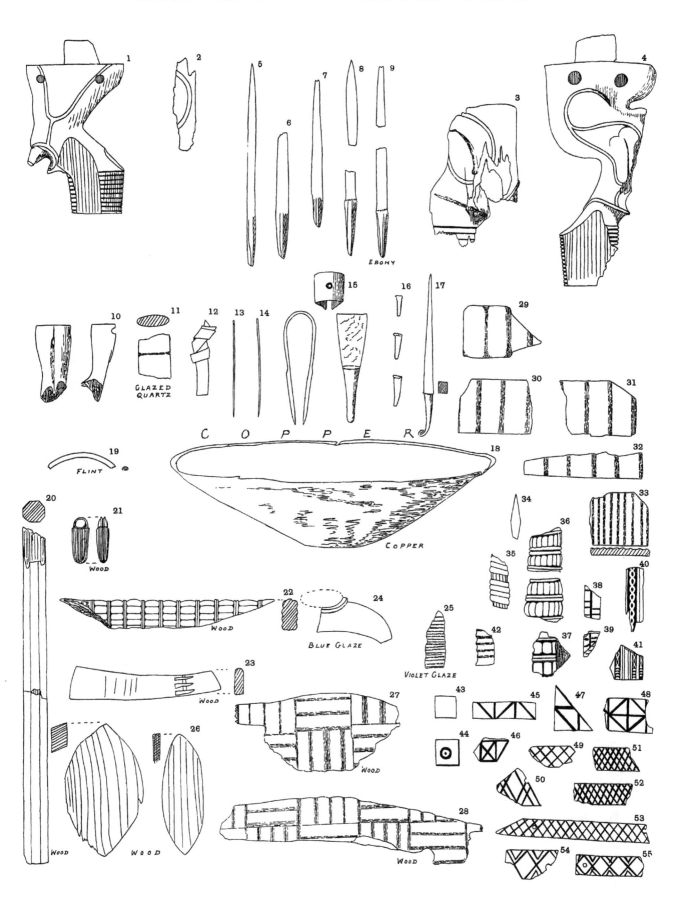

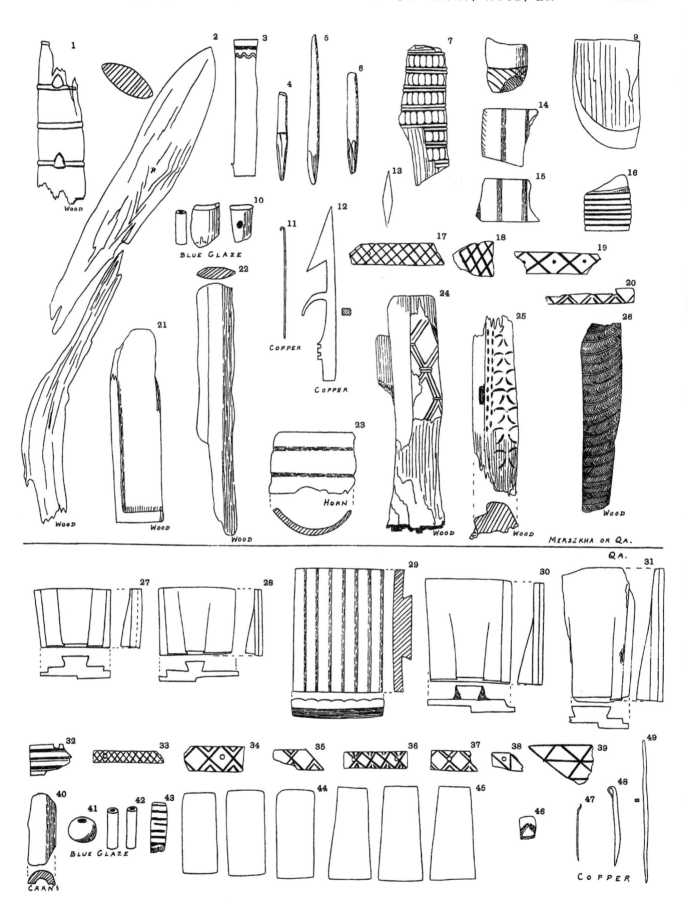

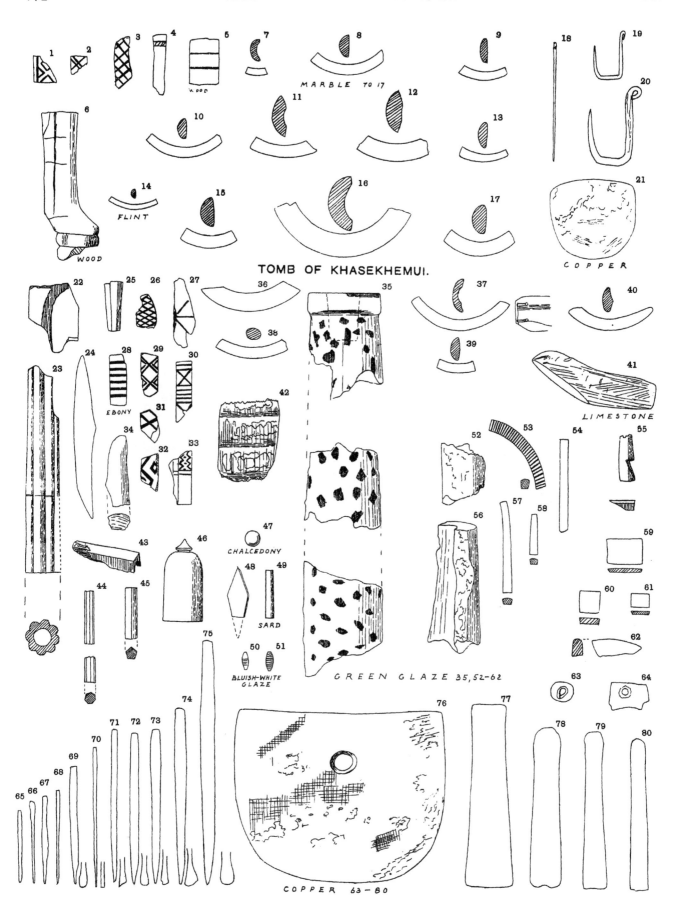

MARBLE TO 17

FLINT

WOOD

COPPER

TOMB OF KHASEKHEMUI.

EBONY

LIMESTONE

CHALCEDONY

SARD

BLUISH-WHITE
GLAZE

GREEN GLAZE 35, 52-62

COPPER 63-80

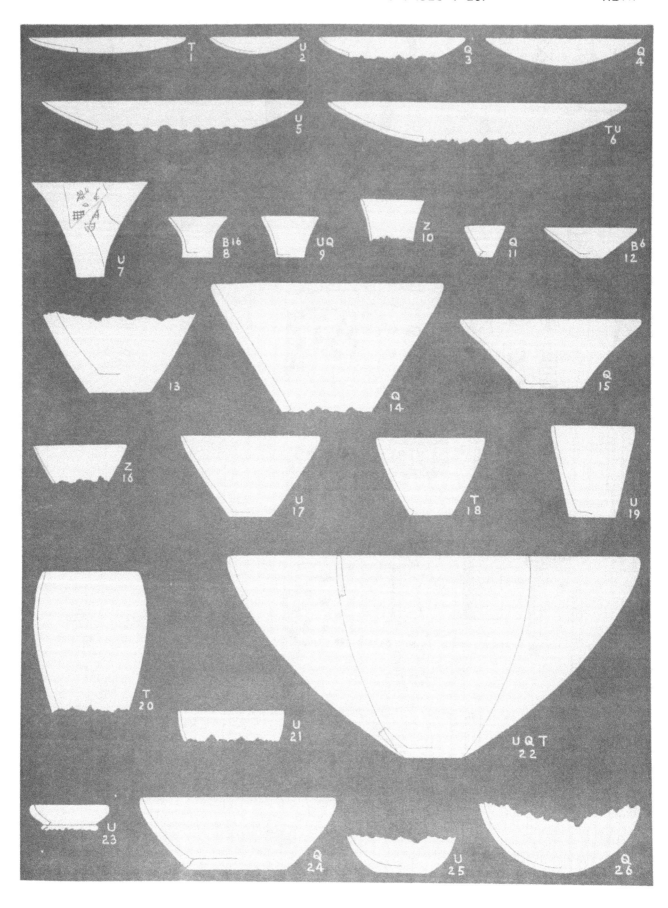

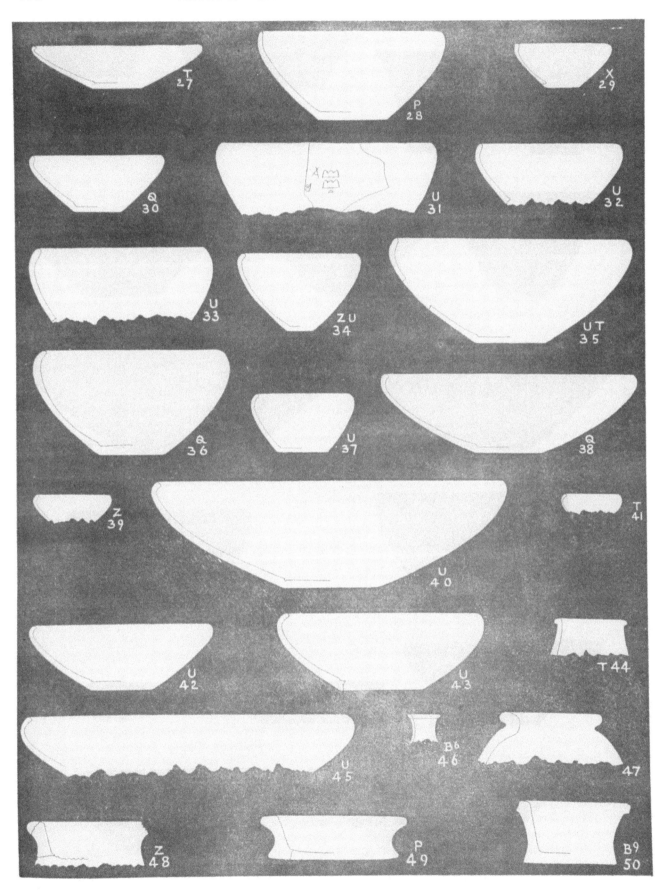

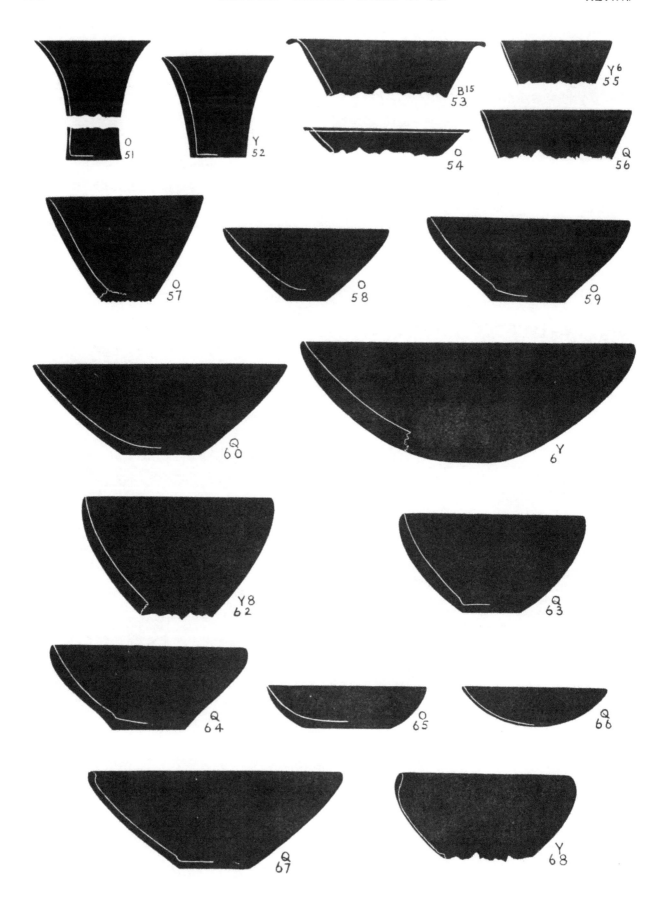

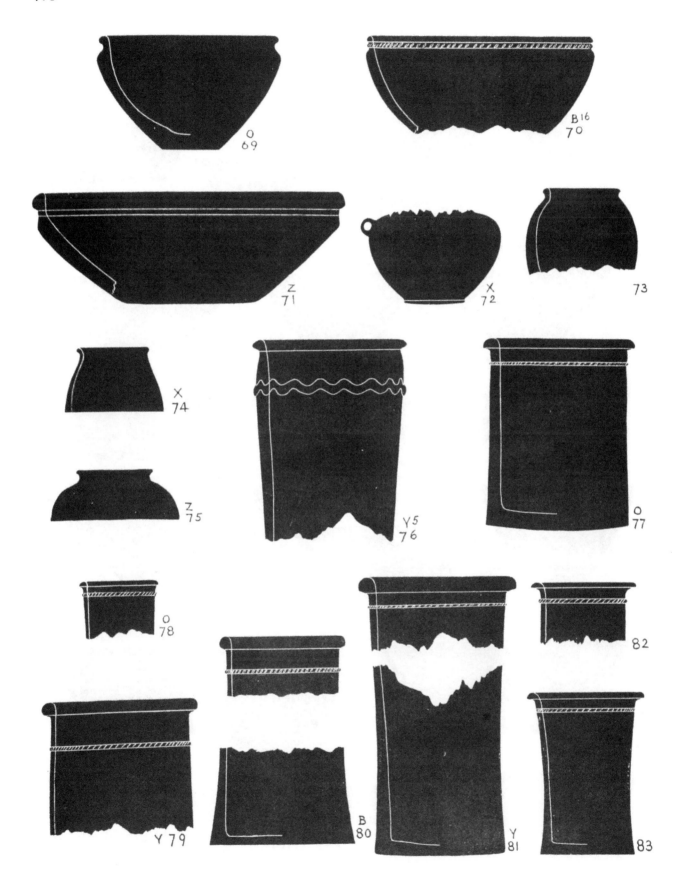

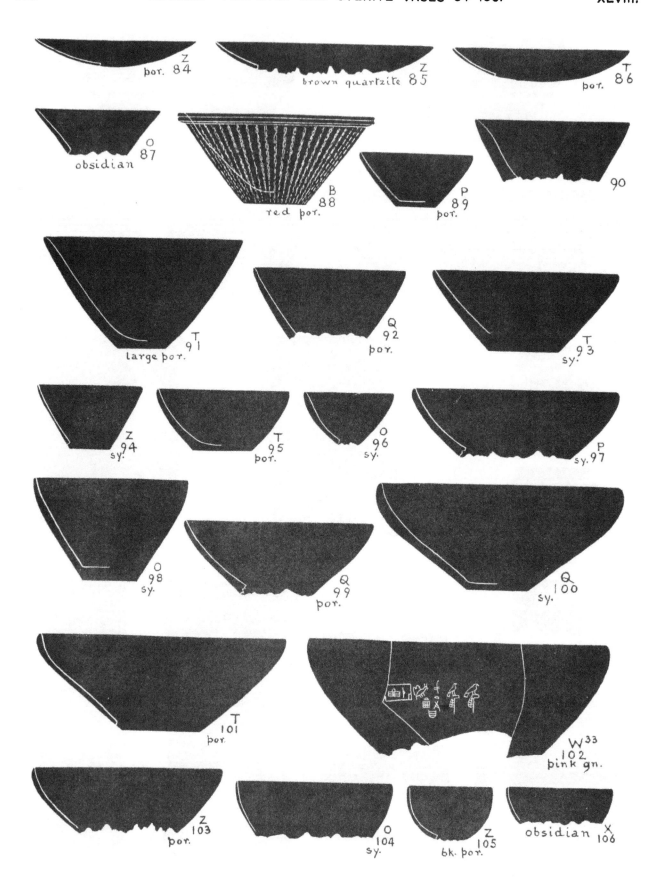

por. 84   Z

brown quartzite 85   Z

T
por. 86

O
obsidian 87

B
88
red por.

P
89
por.

90

T
large por. 91

Q
92
por.

T
sy. 93

Z
94
sy.

T
95
por.

O
96
sy.

P
sy. 97

O
98
sy.

Q
99
por.

Q
100
sy.

T
101
por.

W 33
102
pink gn.

Z
103
por.

O
104
sy.

Z
105
bk. por.

obsidian   X 106

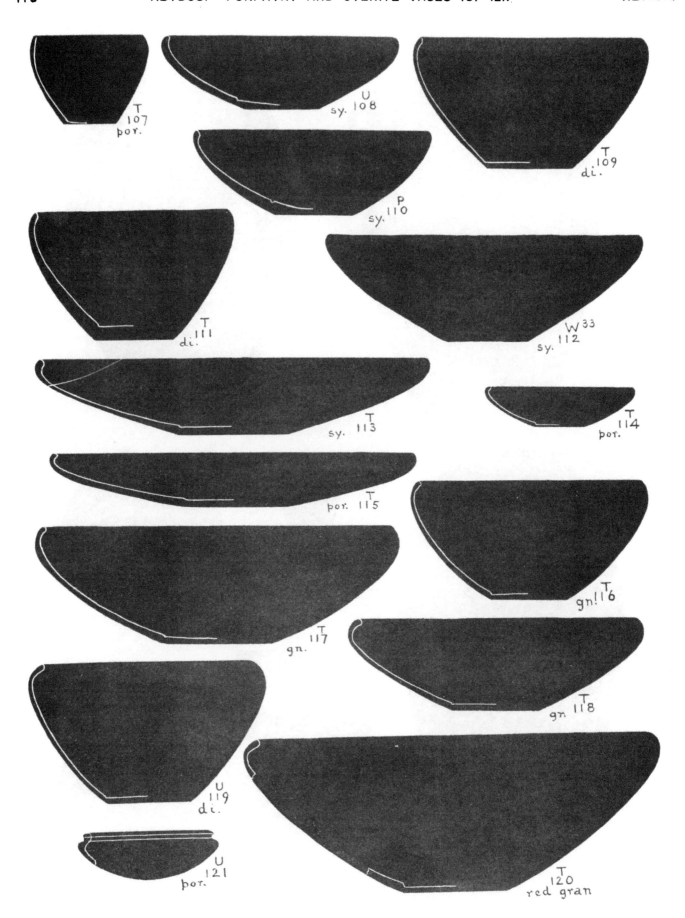

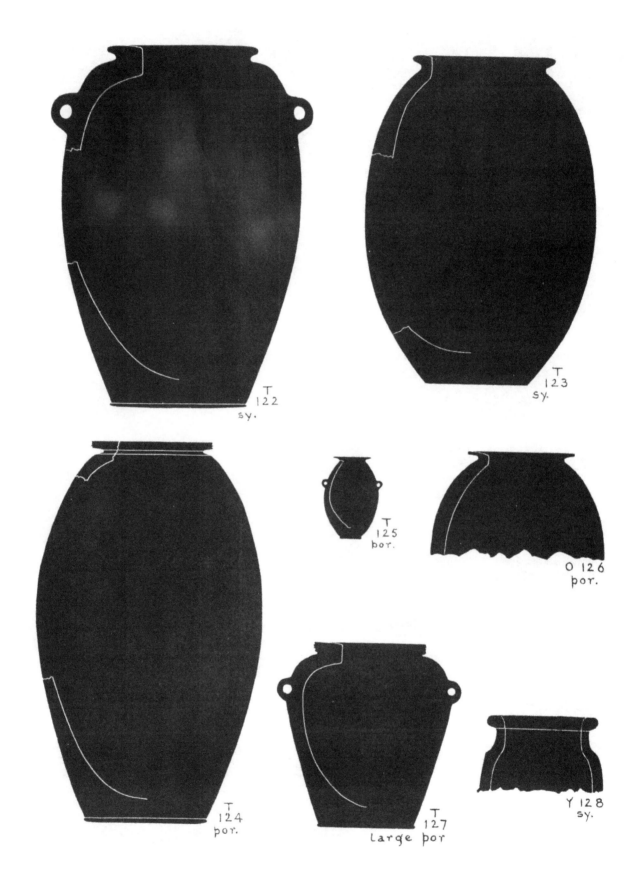

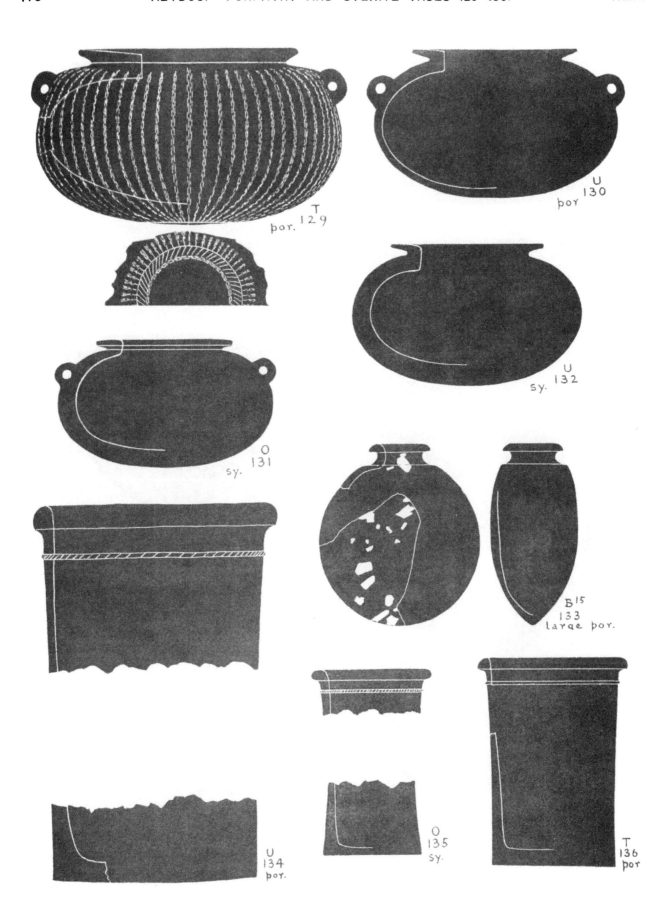

T
por. 129

U
por 130

sy. 131
O

U
sy. 132

B¹⁵
133
large por.

U
134
por.

O
135
sy.

T
136
por

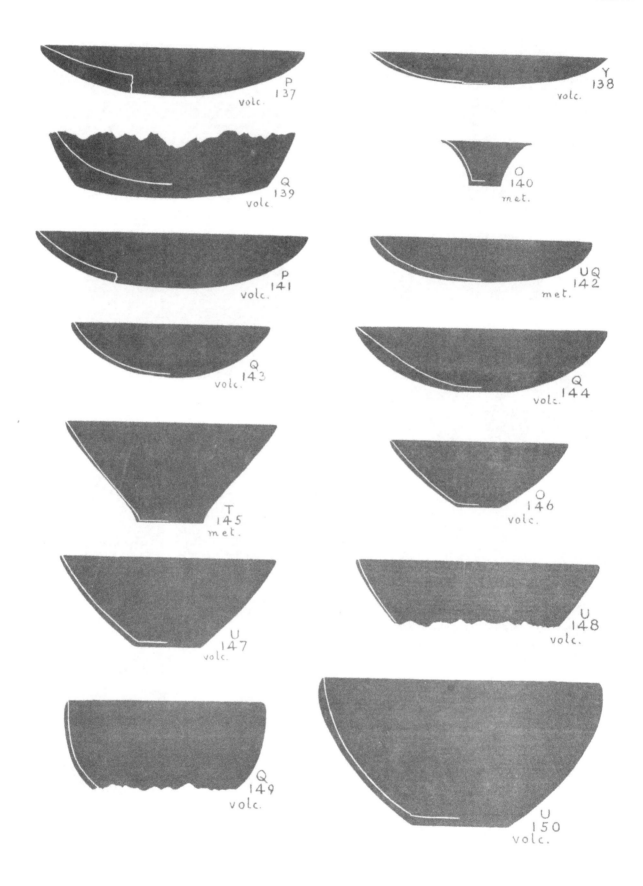

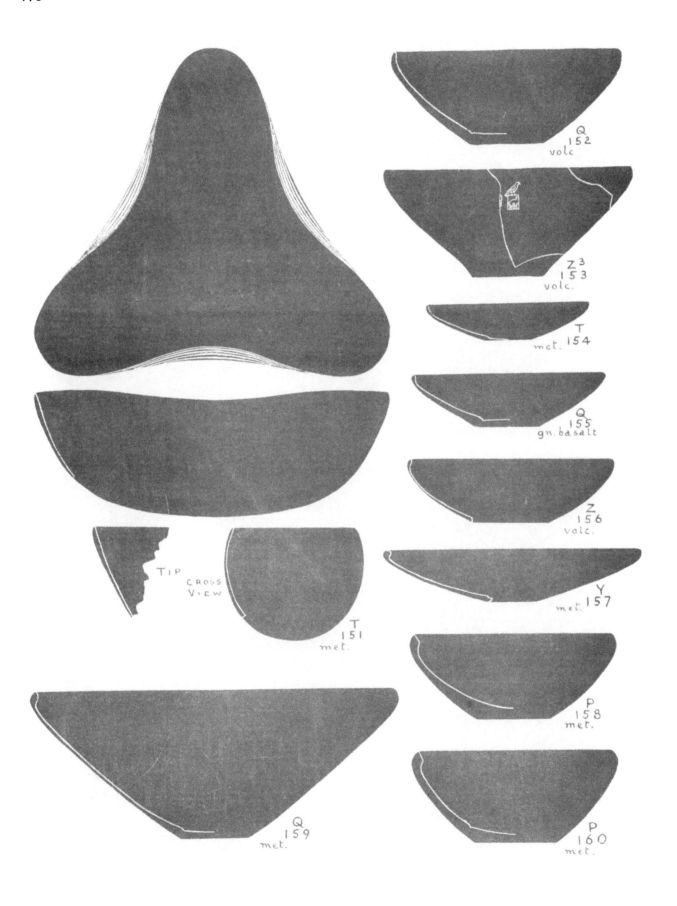

TIP
CROSS
VIEW

T
151
met.

Q
152
volc

Z 3
153
volc.

T
met. 154

Q
155
gn. basalt

Z
156
volc.

Y
met. 157

P
158
met.

Q
159
met.

P
160
met.

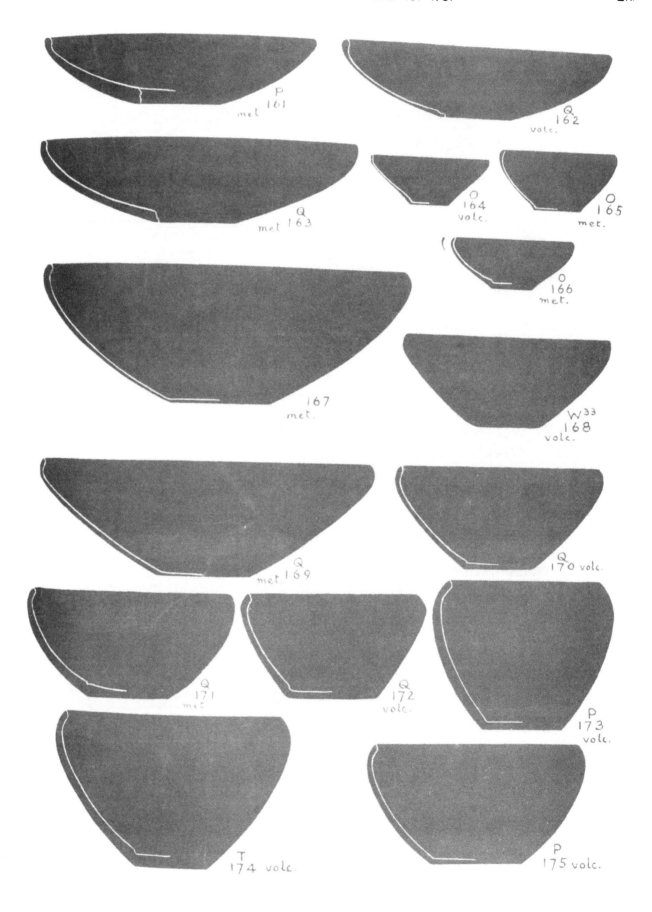

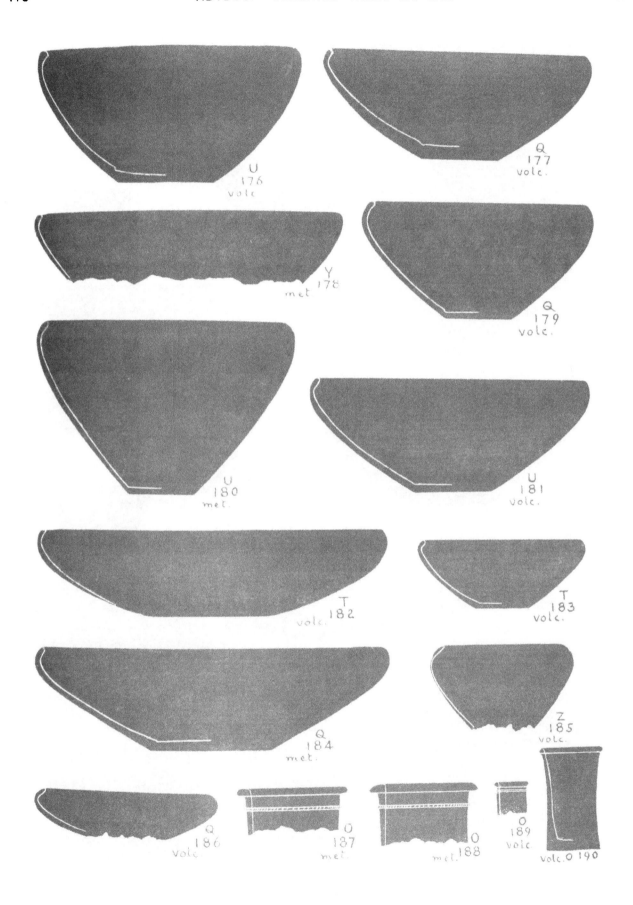

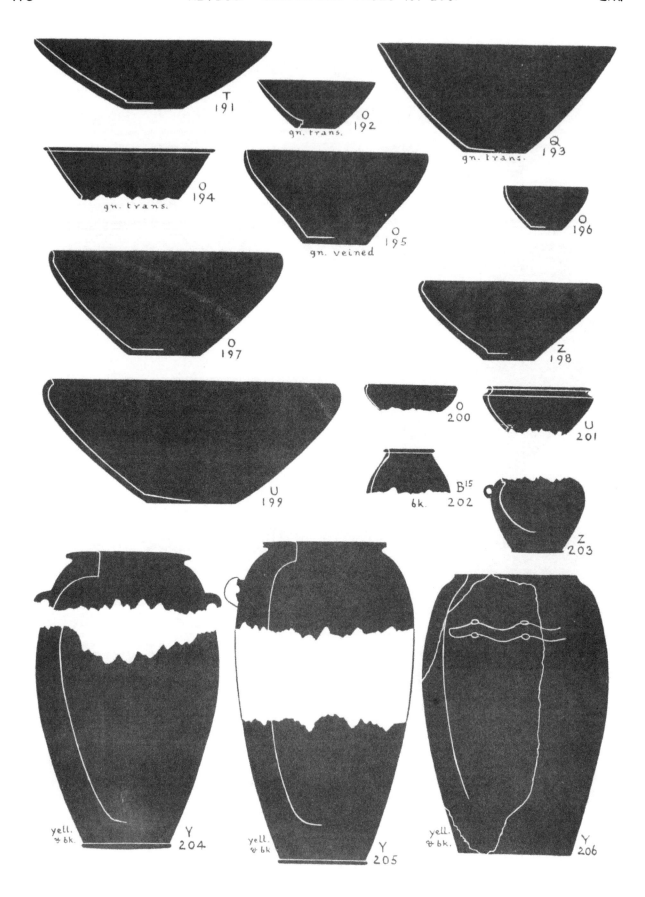

T
191

O
192

gn. trans.

Q
193

gn. trans.

O
194

gn. trans.

O
195

gn. veined

O
196

O
197

Z
198

O
200

U
201

U
199

B[15]
202

6k.

Z
203

Y
204

yell.
& bk.

Y
205

yell.
& bk.

Y
206

yell.
& bk.

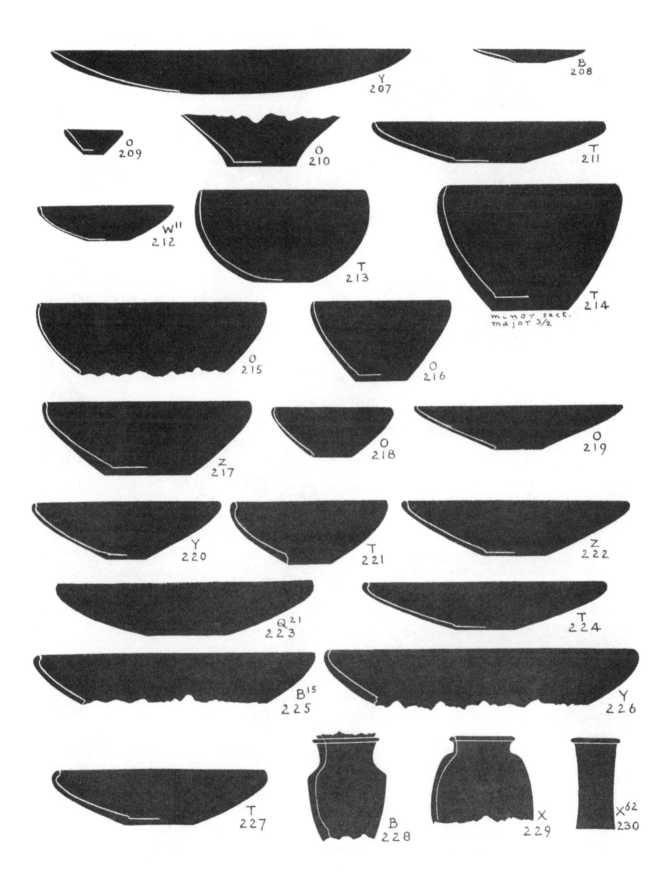

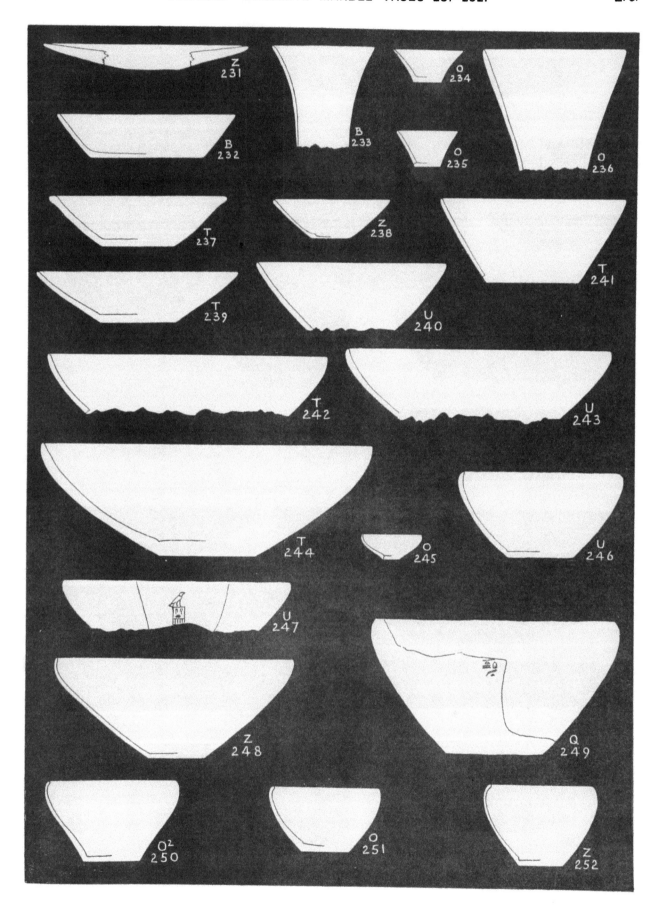

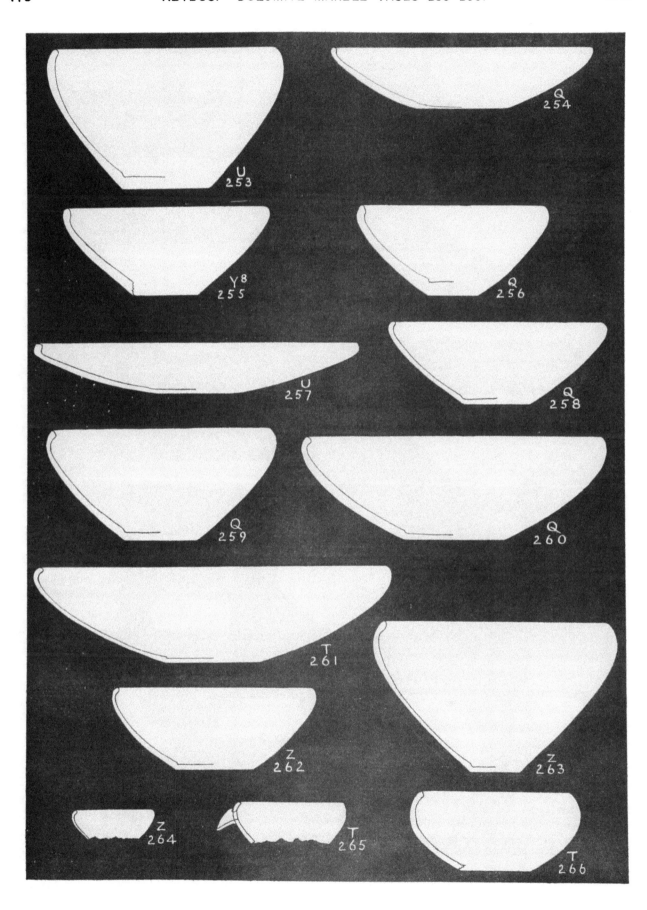

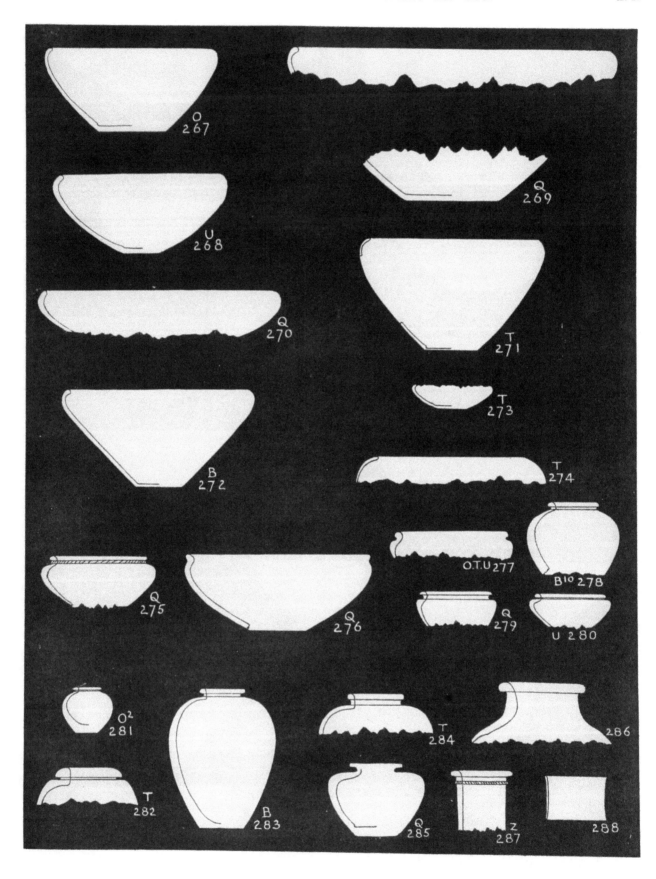

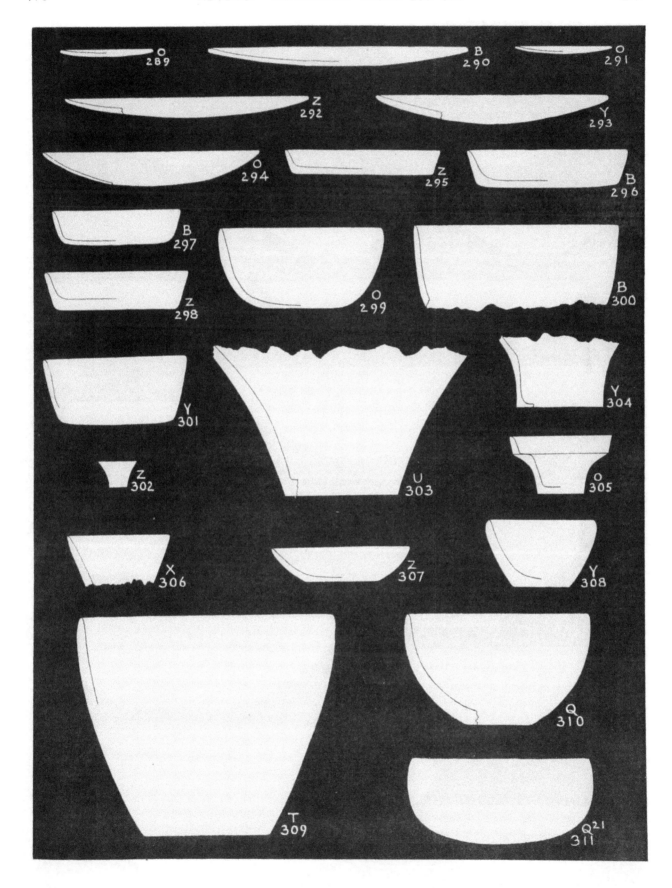

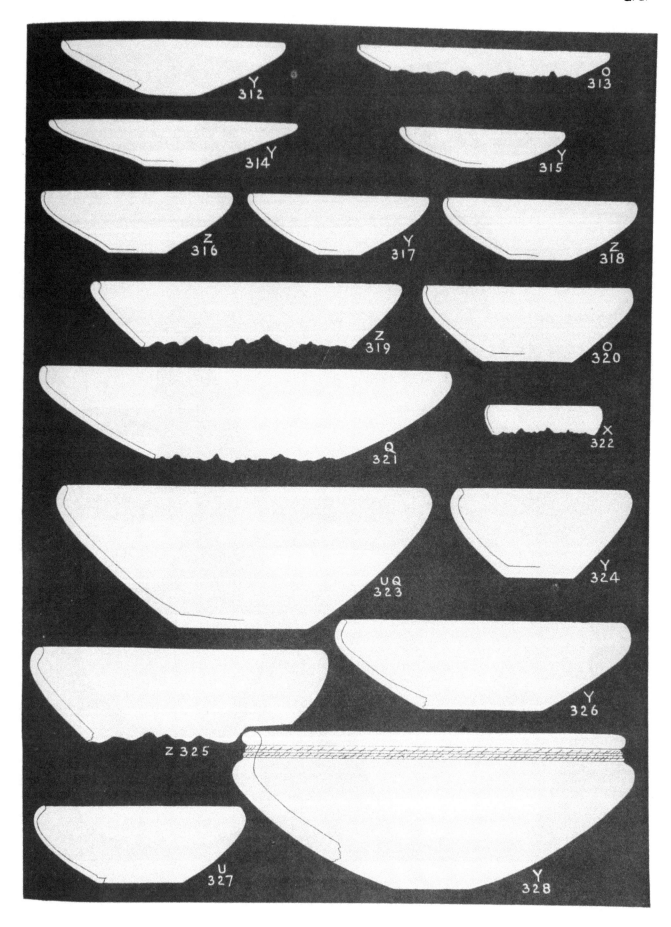

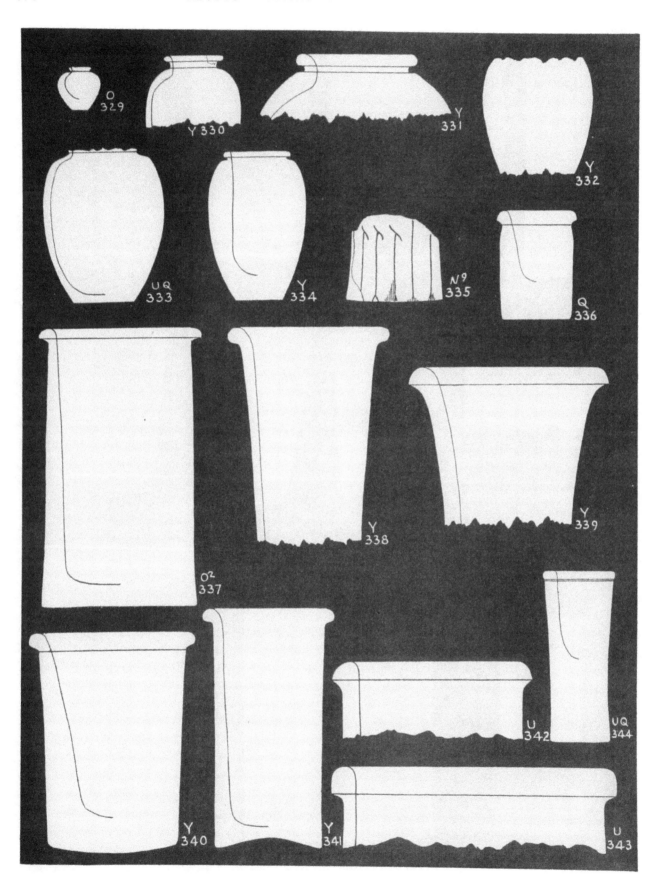

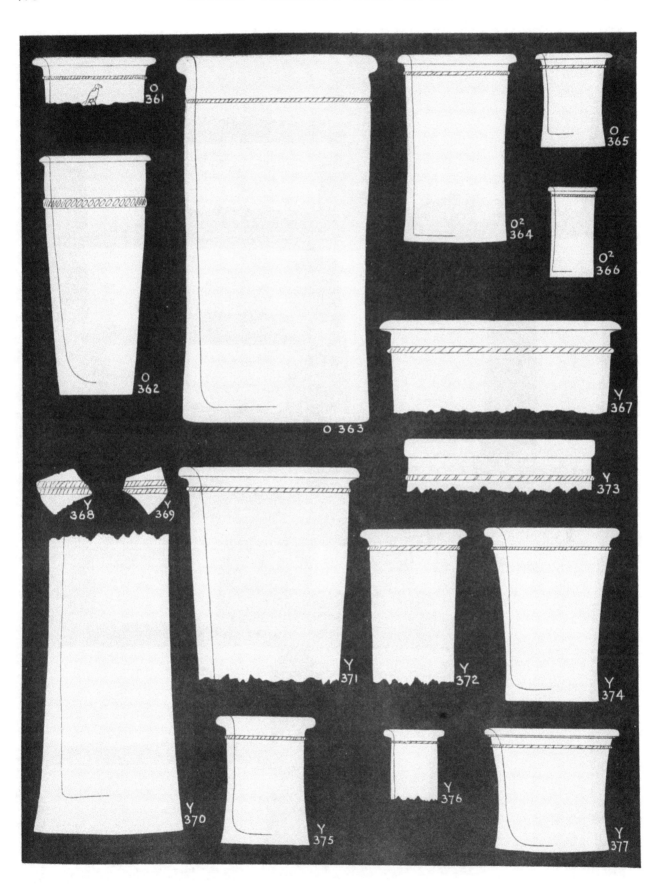

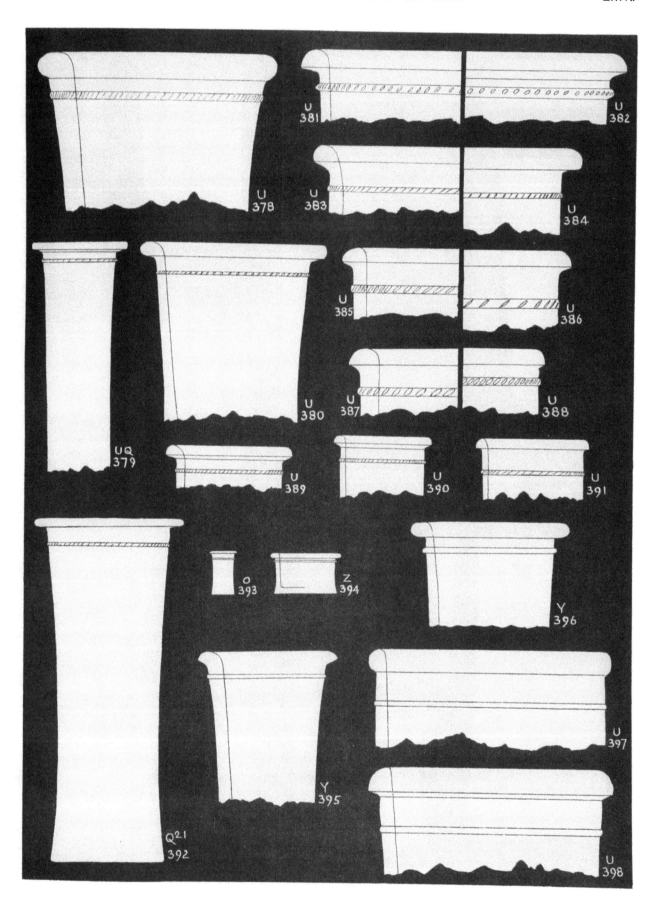

creamy Q 399

lt.br. Q 400

w.calcite red v. Z 401

creamy Z 402

O 403 buff

O 404 yell.

Z 405 pink

O 406 yell.

Z 407 pink & wt.

T 409 gy. red v

B gy. steatite 408

Z 410 wt. red v.

Q 411 gn.gy.

T 412 lt.br.

B pink 414

U 416 breccia

ZY 413 red, wt v.

T red 415

U 417 buff

O 418 buff

O 419

X 420 breccia

O 421 pink

Z 422 purp. striped

T 423 breccia

Z 424 pink & wt

Z 425 creamy

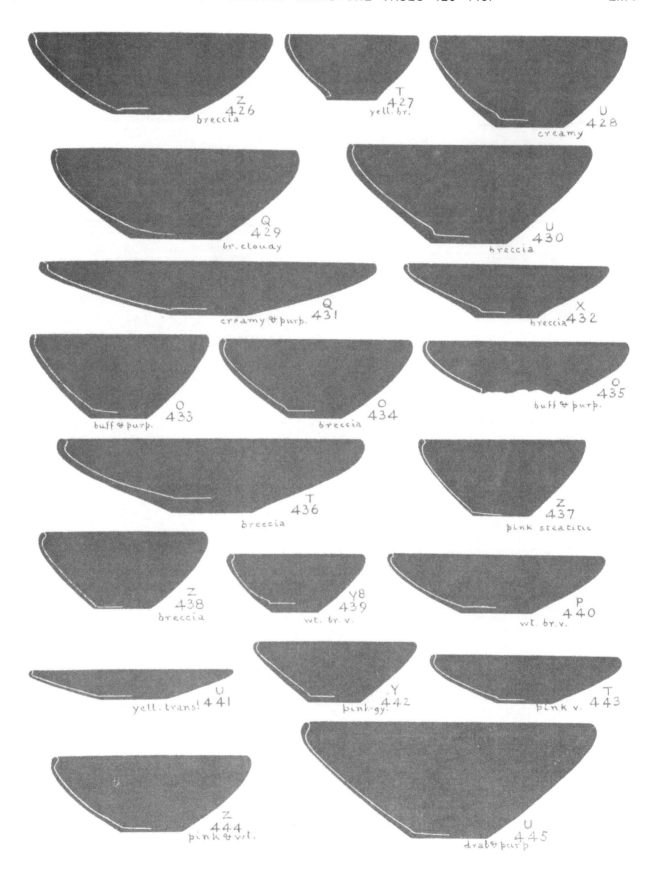

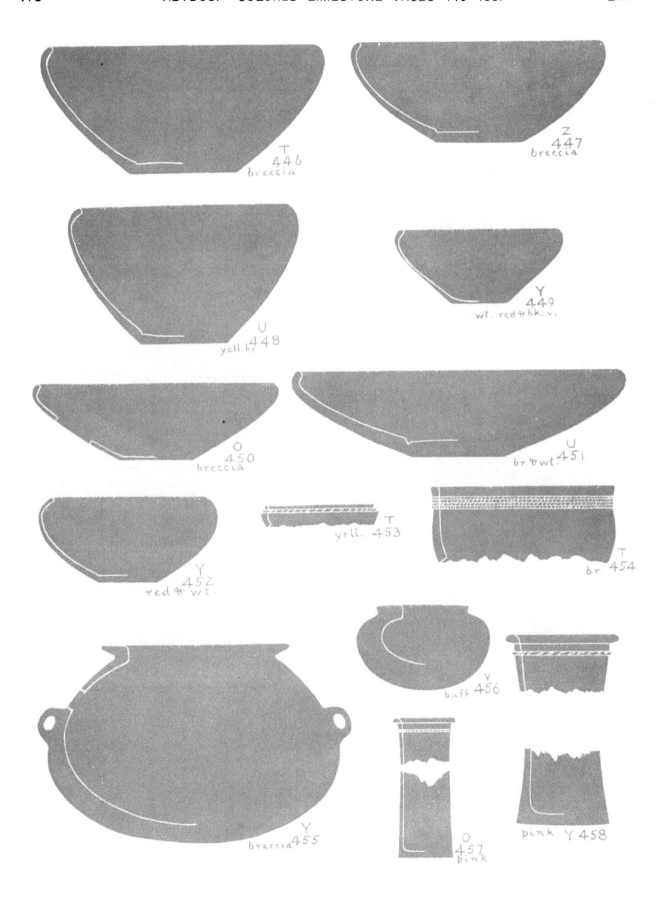

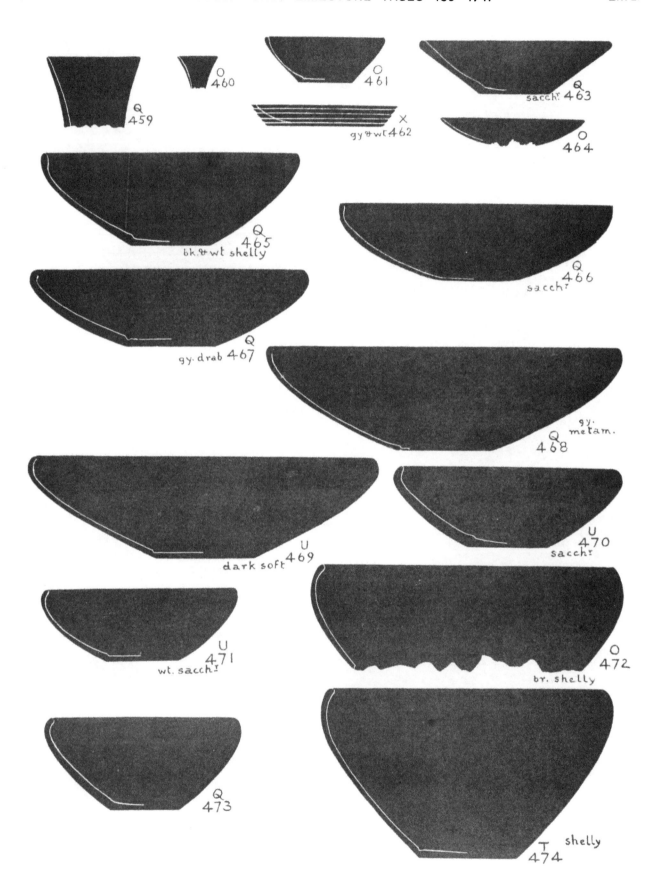

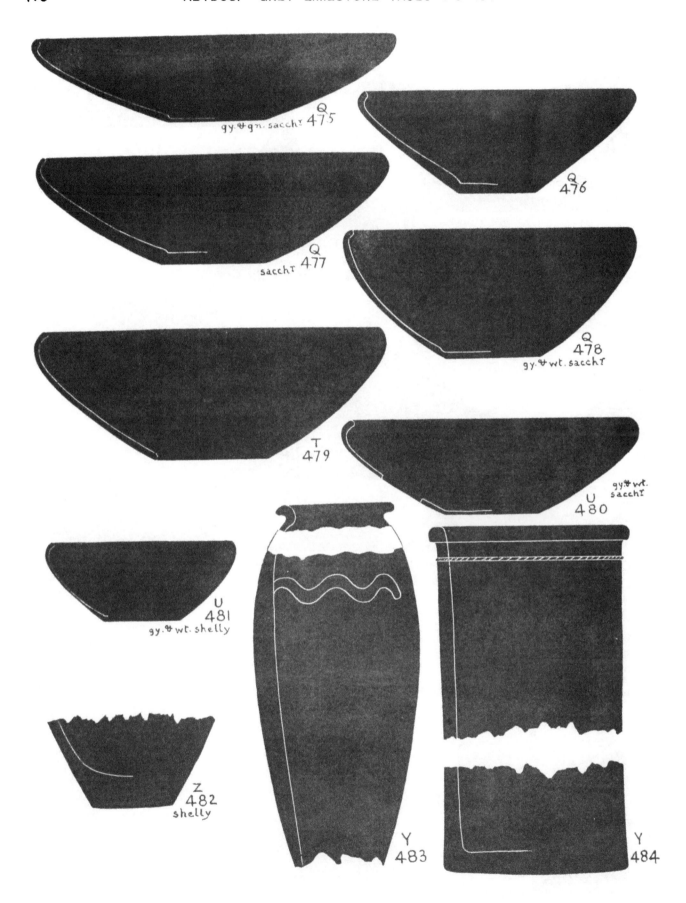

gy.& gn. sacch⊤ 475
Q

Q
476

sacch⊤ 477
Q

Q
478
gy.& wt. sacch⊤

T
479

gy.& wt.
sacch⊤
U
480

U
481
gy.& wt. shelly

Z
482
shelly

Y
483

Y
484

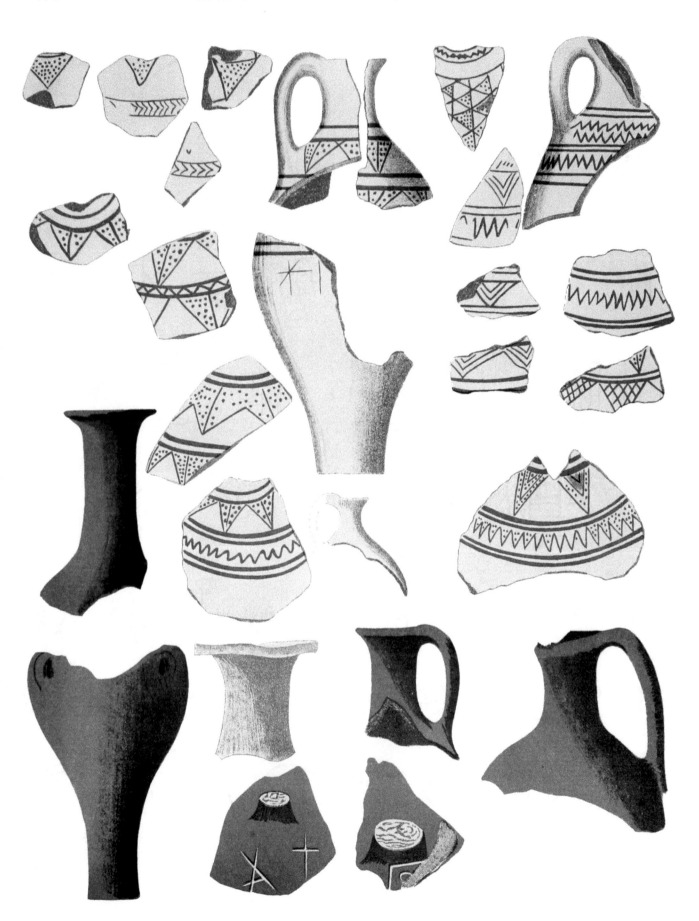

1. TOMB B.10 PERIOD OF MENA.

2. TOMB B.15 PERIOD OF MENA.

3. ZER. STAIRS OF XVIII. DYN.

4. ZER. CHAMBERS OF NORTH SIDE.

5. DEN. TOMB AND STAIRWAY. LOOKING E.

6. DEN. STAIRS AND REBUILT JAMB.

1. DEN. GRANITE FLOOR: TO N.

2. DEN. GRANITE FLOOR: LOOKING S.

3. DEN. STAIR IN S.W. CHAMBER: TO S.E.

4. DEN. STAIR IN S.W. CHAMBER.

5. PERABSEN. N.W. CORNER.

6. PERABSEN. N.E. CORNER.

1. PERABSEN. PASSAGE AROUND TOMB.

2. PERABSEN. CHAMBER, LOOKING N.

3. KHASEKHEMUI. STORE CHAMBERS.

4. KHASEKHEMUI. STONE CHAMBER. TO N.

5. KHASEKHEMUI. STONE CHAMBER, N.W. CORNER.

6. KHASEKHEMUI. DRESSING OF STONE.

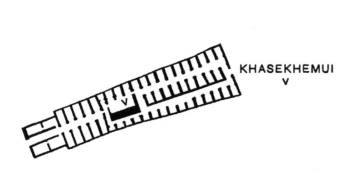

KHASEKHEMUI
V

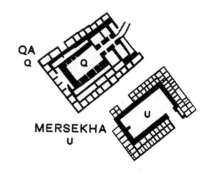

QA
Q

MERSEKHA
U

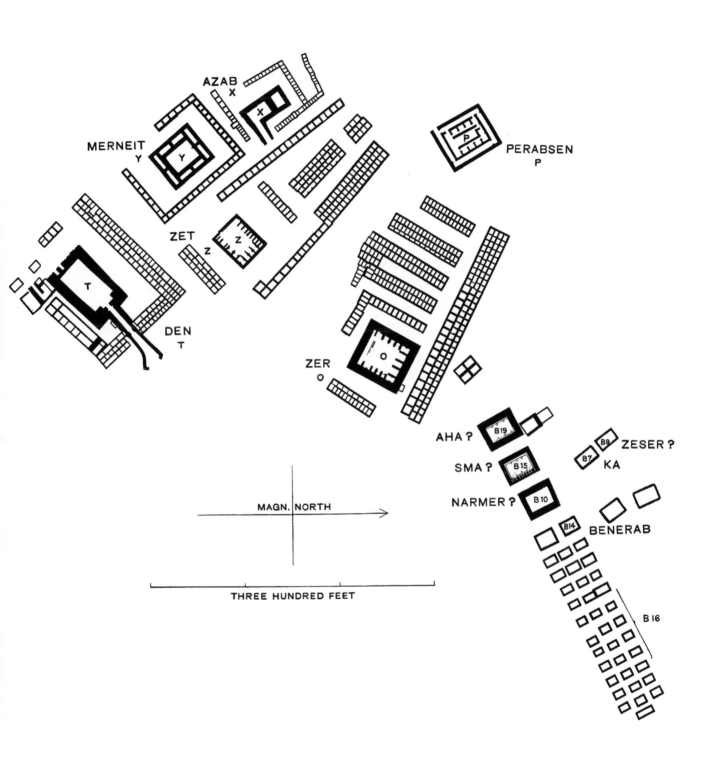

AZAB
X

MERNEIT
Y

PERABSEN
P

ZET
Z

DEN
T

ZER
O

AHA ?

B19

ZESER ?

B8

SMA ?

B15

B7

KA

NARMER ?

B10

BENERAB

B14

MAGN. NORTH

THREE HUNDRED FEET

B 16

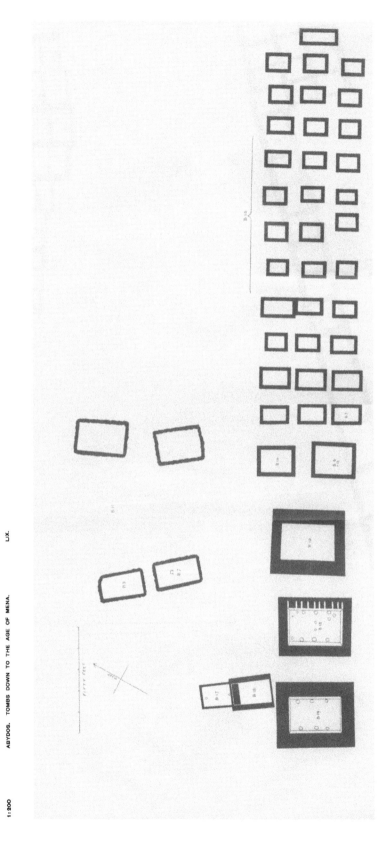

The material originally positioned here is too large for reproduction in this reissue. A PDF can be downloaded from the web address given on page iv of this book, by clicking on 'Resources Available'.

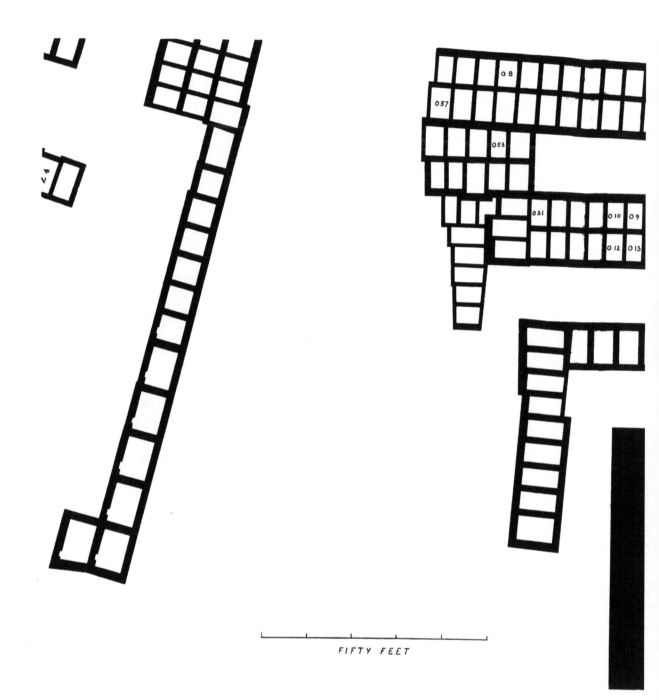

FIFTY FEET

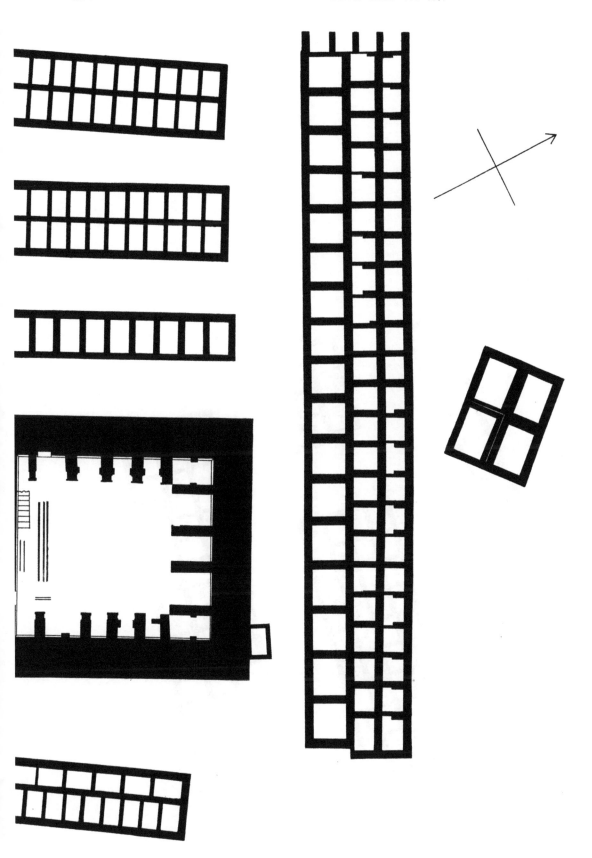

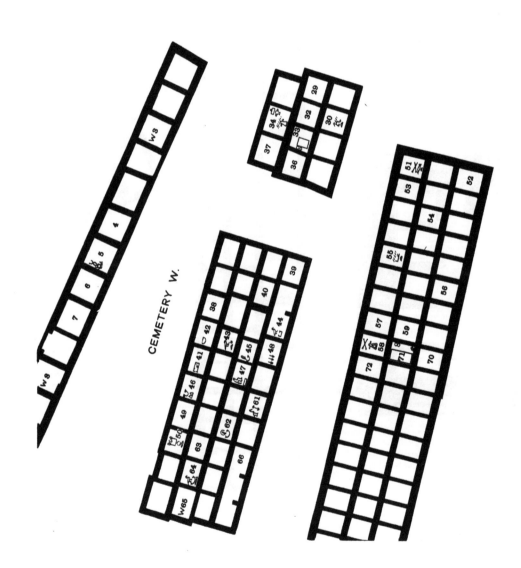

CEMETERY W.

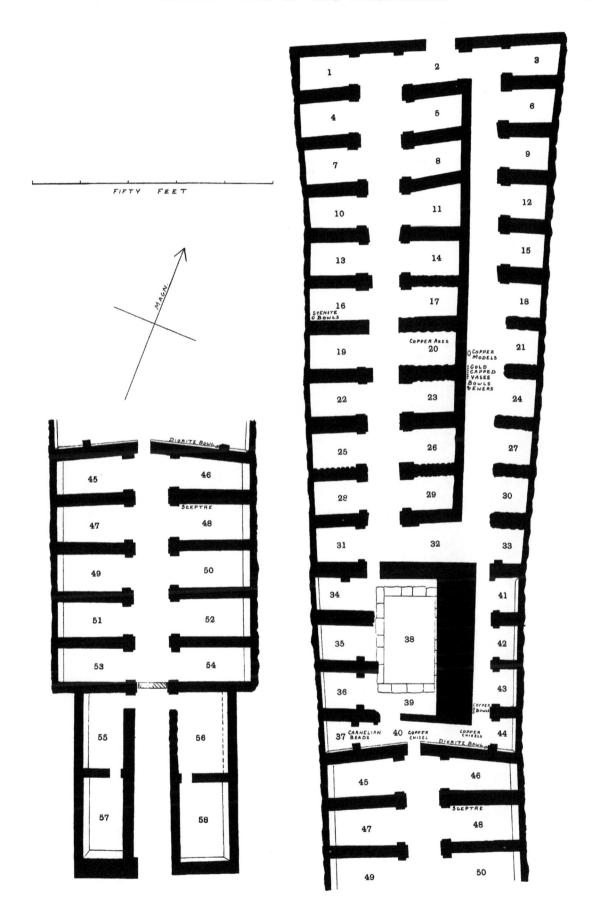

FIFTY FEET

MAGN.

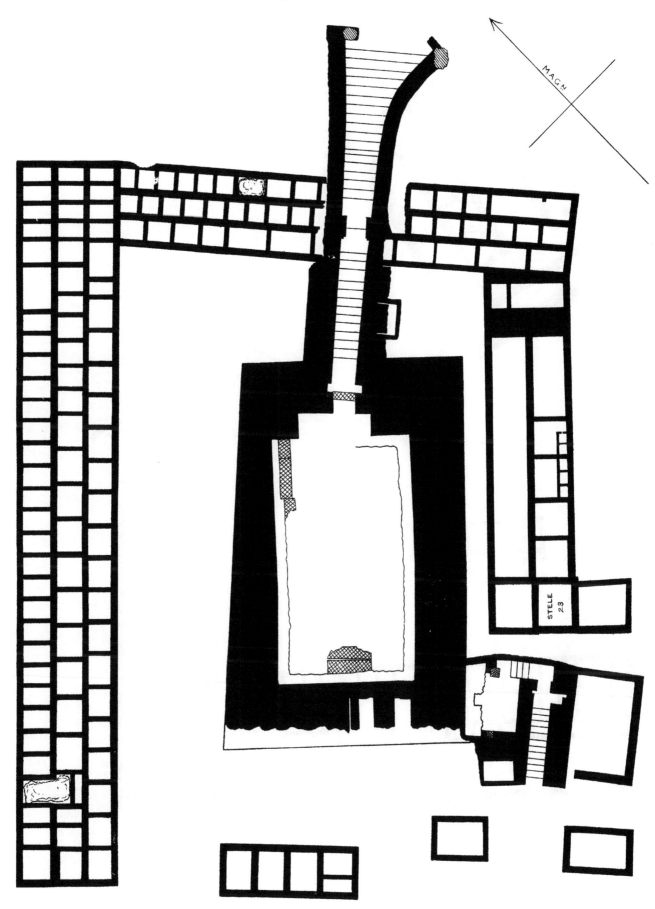

STELE
23

MAGN

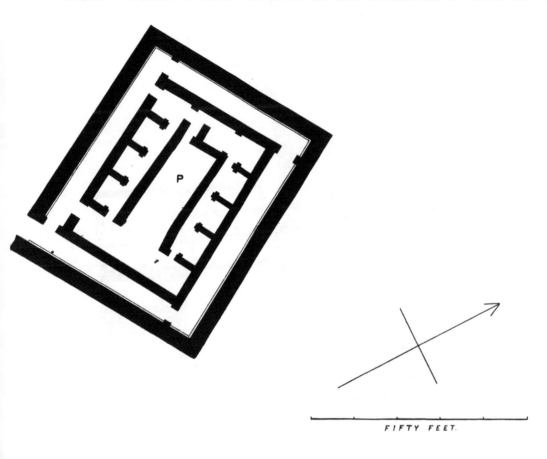

FIFTY FEET.

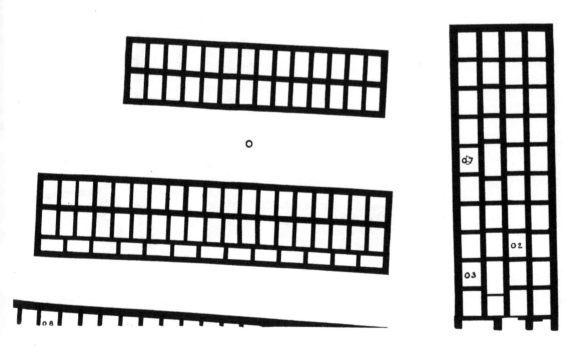

For EU product safety concerns, contact us at Calle de José Abascal, 56–1°,
28003 Madrid, Spain or eugpsr@cambridge.org.

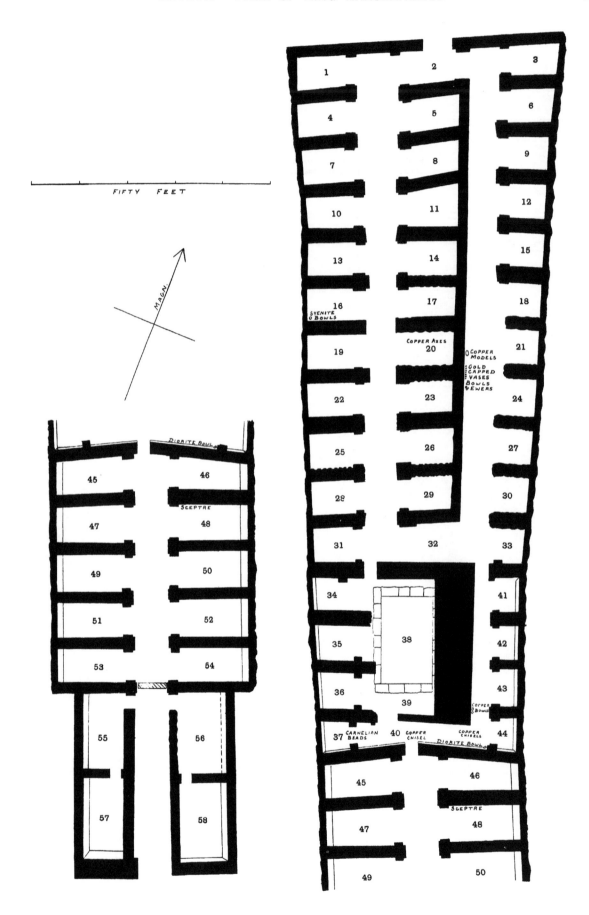